BTEC National Sport
The Student's Practical Guide

Including:
Sport in Society
The Reflective Practitioner
Ethics and Values in Sport
Health and Safety in Sport

Brook Stre'

This book is

Richard Burley, Barry Ryan, Ernst Schute

Published by
Lexden Publishing Ltd
www.lexden-publishing.co.uk

Acknowledgments

We are grateful to the following organisations for granting us permission to reproduce articles, and photographs:

HarperCollins Publishers Inc. for *Slaying the Dragon* by Michael Johnson, © 1996 by Michael Johnson

Photo of basket ball players, page 65, by kind permission of Morris Abernathy, Union University

Photo of rugby players, page 65, by kind permission of Steve Mitchell, www.rugbymatters.net

First Published in 2005 by Lexden Publishing Ltd.

© Richard Burley, Barry Ryan, Ernst Schute

British Library Cataloguing in Publication Data

A CIP record of this book is available from the British Library

ISBN 1-904995-03-9

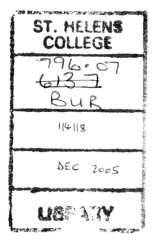

Typeset and designed by Lexden Publishing Ltd

Printed in Malta by Gutenberg Press

Lexden Publishing Ltd
23 Irvine Road
Colchester
Essex CO3 3TS

Telephone: 01206 533164

Email: info@lexden-publishing.co.uk

www.lexden-publishing.co.uk

Contents

Introduction

The purpose of this book is to support sport students in the learning process. Whilst sport is now accepted as an academic area of study, it remains a practical subject and many of you will prefer to learn in an active "hands on" manner. This book will enable you to complete exercises and tasks that will support your lectures and support your understanding of some of the key principles involved in the four core units of the BTEC National programme.

Learning outcomes

All the units in the National Sport course are made up of Learning Outcomes. Each assessment activity is linked to these learning outcomes. These will be abbreviated to **LO** within the text.

Grading criteria

Learning outcomes are linked to the achievement of grading criteria. The grading criteria are divided into **Pass, Merit** and **Distinction**. The depth and quality of your work will determine what grade you can achieve for each assessment and the overall grade for the unit. All pass criteria must be met in order to achieve and pass (in Reflective Practitioner, there are four criteria to meet). The same applies for the merit and distinction criteria. You won't know your final grade until you have completed all assessment activities for each unit, although you will know the type of progress you are making from the feedback received from your lecturers.

How will this book help me pass my course?

This book is to support the work that you do with your tutor. The nature of the exercises within the book are for you to test your understanding as well as practise assessment activities. Ideally, you will use additional information sources such as class notes, text books, web pages, newspaper and magazine articles and CD-Roms to enable you to complete the exercises.

This book should be full of your own notes and thoughts noted during your time on the BTEC National course. The most effective use of this book is that you will go through each unit at your own pace. This can be done at the same pace as your lectures or it could be at your own pace to support your understanding of a topic before going into class. Whichever way you use the book it will be a useful tool to help your learning.

Throughout the book you will have the opportunity to reflect on the knowledge you have developed. Activities will range from formal activities with specific instructions to activities that you can customise to your own circumstances and requirements. Most importantly you will be able to work independently or with support from your lecturing team. The more exercises you complete, the more independently you will be able to work.

How do I pass my course?

Depending on whether you are working towards a National Award, a National Certificate or a National Diploma, you will need to complete 6, 12 or 18 units respectively. Each unit comprises of several learning outcomes and grading criteria.

Features used in this book

The practical ethos of the book is emphasised in the types of exercises that exist for each unit. You will see throughout the book that there are suggestions and recommendations from the authors that will support your work.

These features include:

Tutor talk

The *Tutor talk* boxes represent an opportunity to discuss a specific topic with the subject lecturer. This is especially relevant in the units where up-to-date events and circumstances will be important to your assessment process. Tutor talk will also include the areas in which you may need additional support, e.g. in sourcing relevant statistics for the economic scale of the sports industry or for participatory rates for your sport. Tutor talk will also enable you to refer to you tutor's expertise in a particular area that will help you understand ways in which you can move your work forward and reduce any avoidable barriers or anxieties you may have.

Toolkit

Toolkit is an exercise that will be a practice that will support you in the assessment process. Toolkit will cover the main areas that are part of the grading criteria for each unit and you will be able to check your knowledge and understanding of an area before the any assessment is handed to you. This means that you can work on an assessment with confidence and be clear about the knowledge that you need to demonstrate in each piece of work you produce.

Some activities that go towards building up your knowledge and understanding of the topics covered in the units may include visits to leisure centres, gyms, sports clubs and other types of facilities that are part of the sports industry. It may be the case that your tutor will arrange some trips, but you are expected to arrange visits based on your needs as and when necessary. External speakers may visit you in class to talk about specific issues.

Author's advice

Author's advice is an area in which you can get information from the authors about specific topics. This advice is given with over 50 years worth of sports education experience amongst the authoring team. Typically, Author's advice is based on the experiences witnessed when working with sports students and the typical pitfalls of studying sport. Author's advice will also include general areas of advice linking to academic performance such as tips on effective use of your IT skills and types of tips that will establish a positive impression of your work before the first word is read.

Assessment activities

Throughout each unit, you will come across areas of work entitled *Assessment activities*. These activities link directly to the evidence and information that you need to submit for assessment in order to pass each unit. Each assessment activity links to a Learning Outcome(s) as indicated at the start of each activity.

Weblinks

Throughout each section you will see links to various web pages. These links are available to support your research into the topic areas covered in the text. Additional web links and updates are available from **www.lexden-publishing.co.uk/btecsport**.

Bibliography and references

You will use a wide range of information sources (e.g. text books, interviews, magazine and newspaper articles, reports and Internet sites) throughout your course. It is important that you reference all sources of information both in the text and in a bibliography for each assessment. It is recommended that you talk to your tutor or librarian for support in how to reference work and how to present a bibliography.

Scenario

Some of the assessment activities incorporated into each section are referred to as *Scenario*. A scenario exercise is an opportunity to take general issues and principles and apply them to a specific factual or fictional situation.

Case study

This is a fact-based historic case that looks for you to apply your understanding to real life occurrences in the sports and leisure industries.

Key words and phrases

Each section covers a diverse range of topics. Key words and phrases, such as technical terms, are highlighted in **bold**.

Study tips

File types

Be aware that your college computers may use a different version of Microsoft Word to your PC at home. This may mean that work saved on disk may not be readable by the college machines (this is especially a problem if you are working with a more up-to-date version of Microsoft Word). To get round this avoidable and very frustrating problem, you can save you work in **Rich Text Format (.rtf)** and this means that the work is readable by both machines. To do this, select **Rich Text Format (.rtf)** when saving your work at the **save as type** prompt underneath the file name box. This simple action can save you a lot of time and frustration. You may wish to e-mail your work to a web-based e-mail that is accessible at college or your college e-mail address. The same rules apply to e-mailing work as to saving your work on disk. Finally, don't rely on floppy disks. They can be easily damaged, meaning that your work can be lost. Use CDs or mass storage device that can be connected to a computer via a USB port. Talk to the IT technicians at your college about what they recommend as the most suitable way of transferring work from home to college.

USB storage devices

Presentation of your work

Take the time to present your work as professionally as possible. Produce a front page that details the assignment and unit title, your name, tutor's name and the date you are to hand in your work. Include a contents page that indicates what content is found on which page. To make your contents page accurate and relevant, it is essential to insert **page numbers** into your text. In **Microsoft Word**, this can be done via **insert** on the top menu bar and selecting **page numbers** from the drop down options. An introduction should give a clear explanation of the nature of the assignment. Your main text should be structured in order and you will need to read your work to correct any errors or **typos**, spelling and or grammar. Finally, make sure you use a good quality presentation wallet to hand in. Use the checklist below to help you.

	✓
Front cover	
Contents page	
Introduction	
Main text	
Any additional information	
Bibliography	
Proof read	
Good quality wallet	

You can produce one of these checklists for each of your assignments to help you be more organised and professional in the submission of your work.

Contents

Unit 1: Sport in Society

Introduction to the unit

Unit 1: Sport in Society is a compulsory unit of the National Certificate/Diploma in Sport.

This unit gives you the opportunity to look at how important **sport** has become in our society and explore and investigate why this has happened.

The unit is externally assessed and to successfully complete this you will need to develop important skills that enable you to research information quickly and accurately. These will include organisational skills, interview skills, and information seeking skills.

Aims of the unit

Sport in Society aims to enable you to consider how sport has developed and how it is constantly changing. This will involve looking at the size and importance of the **sports industry** in the modern world. In doing this you will come to understand some of the important **social influences** that have affected your own involvement in sport.

By completing this book you will be fully prepared for the external assessment and feel confident about what you need to do to successfully complete the unit

What the content will cover

Whenever possible the work will focus on you and your sporting interests. Initially you will investigate the **development of sport** and how it is constantly changing. To do this you will need to develop appropriate research skills such as Internet searches, using library resources, writing to external organisations, e.g. governing bodies of sports, visiting local sports facilities and interviewing sports administrators.

Once you understand how it has developed and changed you will then investigate some of the reasons why this has come about. Sport and its development is only a reflection of what is happening in society generally. You will investigate some of these influences and the important issues that face sport in the future. This section will give you the opportunity to research issues and debate them within your group. You will build further research skills such as designing your own questionnaires and doing interviews. It will also provide you with opportunities to bring experts who are working within your community to come and talk about their work. These might include Sports Development Officers, youth leaders and the police.

Next you will research different activities, sometimes called initiatives, that have been developed or are at present being developed to promote the value of sport within the local community, within the country and across Europe. You and your group can get involved in a practical way by supporting a local initiative or in developing your own initiative.

Finally you will be expected to research the size of the **sports industry** and to investigate the employment opportunities that it offers you.

What will I do in class?

There will be a range of different activities that will go on in class and will depend very much upon your tutor/lecturer. These might include formal lectures, class discussions, group work, and role plays to develop your understanding of the unit. What he or she will be keen to develop is your ability to work effectively and independently either as part of a group or individually.

How will I be assessed?

You will be assessed on this unit by completing what is called an **Integrated Vocational Assignment (IVA)**, which is a compulsory part of your qualification. Integrated means that it involves more than one unit of work. In this case your IVA will involve **Unit 3: Ethics and Values**. In this book some of the activities require that you have group discussions or make group presentations. This is really helpful because you can reflect upon other people's ideas. However, the assignment requires that the work you produce is your own original work. So it is really important that after you have worked in a group you must present your own responses to the tasks for assessment.

The **IVA** will cover the following **learning outcomes (LOs)**:

LO1   **Review the development and changing nature of sport**

LO2   **Explore the social influences on sports participation**

LO3   **Investigate the scale of the sports industry**

LO4   **Investigate the role of local, national and European agencies in promoting sport**

What I must submit?

This is an externally assessed unit. That means it will be sent away to be marked by someone other than your tutor. When your tutor feels you are ready and fully prepared he/she will enter you for the assessment. The activities in this book will help in that preparation.

Why sport in society – it's only a game isn't it?

What is sport?

Let's begin by having a clear understanding of what your understanding of **sport** is and also your own understanding of what is meant by **society**. We all agree what sports are or do we?

The reason you are asked this is because what constitutes a **sport** is different for different people. So, for example, some people would argue that an activity such as ballroom dancing is a sport. There are regular competitions held around the country, it demands a high level of skill, there are clearly defined categories of dance and rules that contestants have to abide by and they also have to be pretty fit to compete. It is not much different from more recognised and acknowledged sports such as diving or gymnastics. If ballroom dancing is a sport, does that mean aerobics is a sport? Others would argue it is not a sport because you cannot quantify who wins. You do not have an individual or team winner based around more points/goals scored as opposed to points awarded by some judge, or that one competitor is stronger or faster than another. So is darts a sport? It is very competitive, the winner is decided by who scores a certain amount of points first, there are clear rules; however, it is not particularly physical is it? If darts is a sport does that mean chess is a sport?

Well let's see if, as a group, you can agree what makes up a sport with a debate called **'defend the indefensible'**.

Remember before you start the debate to draw up your own thoughts with examples of what constitutes a sport. Then at the end reflect on other people's ideas and if you agree with them add them to your own list.

 Toolkit : Defend the indefensible

The International Olympic Committee has decided for the 2012 Games, there is room for one more sport. Ballroom dancing, golf, skate-boarding, darts, aerobics, snooker and fishing are being considered. Take any two from this list. In the debate half the group are to make the case for one of the activities and vice-versa.

At the end of the debate draw up your conclusion about what constitutes a sport by completing the table below:

Characteristics of sport	Examples
Rules	Forward pass in rugby

What is society – I can do what I want can't I?

Communism, capitalism, the mixed market are all different types of society. **Society** can have different meanings for different people. The former Prime Minister of Britain, Mrs Thatcher, is quoted as saying:

"There is no such thing as society. There are individual men and women and there are families."
Margaret Thatcher (1989)

However, there is clearly something that glues together these people into groups, creates some sense of identity, allows them to interact and live interdependently. As in sport there must be some rules that are based on beliefs and values that we all sign up to enable us to live relatively harmoniously. It is important to be clear about **what you think** society means.

The next activity is going to give you the opportunity to practice your interview skills in a relatively safe and secure environment with people you know. When interviewing someone it is important to be clear about the information you require from them. The interview needs to be planned and structured. There should be an introduction, the questioning period and a conclusion. The questions will need to be clearly phrased. To start with pre-plan a number of questions that you think will draw out from your interviewees the information you require. When planning your questions keep them very simple and very open. Questions that are designed to get more than a simple yes or no response are often referred to as **open questions**.

Toolkit : Important characteristics of society

Interview your tutor, your parents, grandparents and friends to draw up a list of important characteristics that make up a society.

1.
2.
3.
4.
5.
6.

What is a Community Sports Development Officer?

Specific employment opportunities have emerged that recognise and promote the role and increasing importance of sport and physical activities in our society. Most local authorities employ people to develop and promote sport within their locality. You are asked to play the role of a **Community Sports Development Officer** and you will be asked to undertake a variety of tasks that any development officer might be asked to complete in their work to support local clubs in developing sport within their region. An understanding of this role will be important if you are to successfully complete your **IVA**.

These tasks might include providing reports back to your line manager, improving links between local schools and local sports clubs, assisting clubs to accessing funding for their projects, developing awareness and promoting the principles, values and ethics associated with sport.

Toolkit: What does a Community Sports Development Officer do?

What does a Community Sports Development Officer do? Create a job description for yourself and then add this to the outline on the following page.

Tutor talk

How will you find out about this? There are a number of different sources of information you could use. Start by asking your tutor if he/she knows anything about the job. It would be helpful if a local Community Sports Development Officer could come to talk about his/her role.

Author's advice

A job description describes the duties and responsibilities that are involved in a particular job, in this case as Community Sports Development Officer. The information that you include in the job description might include the following:

- job title
- where the job is located
- key purpose of the job
- general responsibilities
- special areas of responsibilities.

Job Description

Job Title:

Location:

Key Responsibilities:

- Sports development officers will work in partnership with a wide range of organisations to utilise local resources and build on any regional or national initiatives.

-

-

General Responsibilities

The variety of activities that a sports development officer could become involved with includes:

- identifying sports, recreation and health initiatives.

-

-

-

-

-

Areas of Special Responsibilities

A specialised post, such as a disability sports development officer, may include:

- training and educating coaches, volunteers, facilities staff, etc, in disability issues. Experts in disability awareness may well be called on, where appropriate.

-

-

-

Section 1: How things have changed

LO1:   The development and changing nature of sport

At the end of *Section 2* you will be asked to prepare **a report** for local clubs on the sports industry. *Section 1* covers the **historical development of sport**. You will examine the **changing nature of sport** in *Section 2*.

> ## Author's advice
>
> In the main body of the report you need to gain some understanding of how sport has developed and changed in Britain over the past 200 years.

Education···Education···Education

One important factor that you are probably able to identify through your own experiences is the role of education and in particular **physical education**. In the development of modern sports and the values that underpin the way we play sports. You will be looking more closely at these values in **Unit 3: Ethics and Values**.

Public schools and the development of modern sports

Sport is played all over the world. However, in early times there were no sports as we know them today. Sports emerged from a range of different sources. Some of our sports can be traced back to ancient Greece and Rome, some emerged from survival and military activities, e.g. fencing, archery and horse racing, and other sports came out of simple play or recreational activities.

Britain is often referred to as "the crucible of modern sport". Many of the easily recognisable sports such as football, rugby and hockey were developed in Britain during the 19th century and they had their roots in pre-industrialised, popular recreational activities, often referred to as **mob-games**. These were very local, often very violent, had no written rules, no restricted area of play, no set number of players and were often linked to pagan or early Christian festivals. Even today on Shrove Tuesday in Ashbourne, Derbyshire a game of mob football is played by the local inhabitants.

In the early development of sports as we know them today the **public schools** in particular were very important. The principle characteristics of a public school in the 19th century: it was for the well to do, expensive, predominantly boarding, independent of the state but neither privately owned and not profit making. *Mangan* (2000) defined them as "independent, non-local, predominantly boarding schools for the upper and middle classes". Perhaps the best known public schools are Eton, Harrow, Rugby, Winchester, St. Pauls and Merchant Taylor's. However, the 19th century was a period of great expansion of public school education and these schools played a vital role in the development of the rules, the establishment of governing bodies for particular sports and the organisation of many modern sports.

Organised team games and activities such as football, cricket and rowing, if situated near a river, were to become an integral part of the character training of successive generations of young middle and upper class gentlemen. Reforms within the public schools during the early 19th century led to the ideals of **athleticism** and **muscular Christianity**, which reflected the moral integrity and physical endeavour considered desirable for future leaders of commerce, the army, the church and colonial administrators.

The ideals of: healthy body, healthy mind, of playing within the rules, that taking part was more important than winning, working for the team were all values, and beliefs that were considered important for future leaders at home and in the developing British Empire. However, public schools did not only use physical activity and sport to promote these values, they were also vitally important in transforming traditional folk/mob games such as **hurling** or **knappen** into the modern sports of association such as football, rugby and hockey we know today. Old boys from these schools were instrumental in taking these games out into the wider social world as well as being responsible for establishing governing bodies for the organisation of the sports.

What you should appreciate by now is that whilst sports are in the main enjoyable physical activities, the type of activities you participate in have been **socially constructed**. One of the facts that you will have become aware of from your lessons, reading and discussions is that in a relatively short period of time there have been a great many social and physical changes. These may include general social factors such as better and easier transportation, the shorter working week and therefore more leisure time, more disposable incomes.

Toolkit: Factors changing sport

Using the table below identify in note form how the listed factors have changed sport and suggest reasons why they have been so important.

Factors that have changed sport	How have they changed the sport?	Why do you think this has happened?
Increase in leisure time	More people participate in sports of their choice.	Improved productivity means that people are able to work fewer hours but still earn enough to participate in their chosen sports.
Improved public transportation systems		
More disposable income		
Increased car ownership		
Increased life expectancy		
Globalisation		
Education for all		
World Wars		
Equality of opportunities		

Author's advice

Do not just guess what the factors changing sport might be.

- Go and talk to people of different ages involved in playing, coaching or running these activities.
- The local authority will be able to give your information on provision and participation. Often they produce useful contact publications.
- Use your contact with your governing bodies.
- Go to the Sport England website **www.sportengland.org**. Take your time here and explore this source as you will find it useful for other research you need to do.
- Two other useful websites are the **Skills Active** and the **DCMS** sites **www.culture.gov.uk**.

Then there are also some very sport specific factors such as the development and role of governing bodies of sport, the role of physical education in schools, growth of sports academies, specialist sport schools and colleges. These changes have led to exciting career opportunities within the sports industry.

Development of state school education

In the 19th and 20th centuries not all young people, and particularly working class children, were given the opportunity to attend a public school. In the 19th century many working class children were working from the age of five in the cotton and wool mills or in the factories and steel works that had become established during the Industrial Revolution. They could be working up to 50 or 60 hours a week. Indeed, compulsory education for all children was not introduced until near the end of the 19th century when there started to develop what is known as a state system of education. It was the *Forster Act, 1870* that made education for all children between five and 13 years compulsory and it also saw the first development of **physical education** in elementary schools. However, the experience of young children in these schools was much different from those young boys who went to public school. Today the framework for PE in state schools is provided by the **national curriculum** but this has not always been the case and if you were a pupil at the beginning of the 20th century your experience would have been entirely different. The first nationwide syllabus for **physical training** (**PT**) was established in 1902. Since then their have been a number of new syllabi introduced that gradually moved the curriculum from **PT** to **physical education** (**PE**).

Toolkit : A time line of the development of PE syllabi in state schools

Below is a timeline of syllabi for PT/PE in state schools. By completing the timeline, you will get a feeling for what PE would have been like at different times in the 20th century.

SYLLABI OBJECTIVES

e.g. Improve fitness and discipline

| 1902 | 1904 | 1909 | 1919 | 1933 | 1952/53 | 1988 |

SYLLABI CHARACTERISTICS/ACTIVITIES

e.g. Military drill

Toolkit: Role play activity

Create a five minute practical session for your group from one of the early syllabi and then lead your group in doing it. Then discuss the main differences from your own experiences.

Useful sources of information for you would be one or more of the PE/sports textbooks.

As you know, PE takes place in schools, colleges and universities. However, it is a broad concept with many interpretations that cover practical skill development, social development and preparing you to continue activity when you leave school. In Britain there is no fully centralised system of PE and even with the national curriculum no two schools do exactly the same things. However, PE and sport in schools is often the first opportunity that young people have to get involved in organised sport. Today they are considered an important aspect of the education system. In the Government report, *Raising the Game*, school sport is recognised as the single most important aspect in the development of sporting opportunities for the nation because it touches the life of every child.

Toolkit: Definitions and objectives of physical education and sport

Work in small groups or individually.

1.   Define what you mean by the physical education and sport:

•   Physical education is _____

•   Sport is _____

2.   What are the key objectives of physical education?

•   _Development of individual skills across a range of activities_

•   _____

•   _____

•   _____

•   _____

Author's advice

Key objectives really highlight the main purposes of physical education.

Toolkit: Definitions and objectives of physical education and sport (continued)

3. As a group or individually, document the types of sports experiences you have had and classify them according to the national curriculum areas of activities. Draw this up in the table below.

Games activities	Gymnastic activities	Swimming/water safety	Athletic activities	Adventure activities

Toolkit: Definitions and objectives of physical education and sport (continued)

4. Discuss whether the experience of all within the group was of a balanced programme of activities that included team orientated, individual, competitive and non-competitive movement-based activities?

5. Identify the important factors that influenced their choice of activities. For example, did the interests of their teachers affect those opportunities? Was what they did limited by where they lived or the facilities of the school?

6. Review your objectives of PE and identify how these were being met.

7. Compare what you did in your school with the experiences of someone who was at school before 1939 and someone who was at school in the 1960s. A good film to look at to give you an idea of school PE in the 1960s is **Kes**; the PE scene gives some interesting insight into the unstructured approach to PE.

Tutor talk

In order to complete this table you will need to talk with your PE tutor to find out how activities are classified. Another useful source for you is the national curriculum website: **www.nc.uk.net**. It is worthwhile interviewing people from different eras to see what their experiences were. Parents and grandparents are good sources of information. Ask them about the facilities that were available, the range of activities, the type of equipment they used and how often they played. They might have some pictures of themselves playing sports they would be prepared to lend you.

Much closer links are now being developed between school sport and sports clubs. **PE, School Sport & Club Links** (PESSCL) is a joint **DCMS/DfES** initiative to implement a national strategy for PE and school sport.

DCMS = Department for Culture, Media and Sport (**www.culture.gov.uk**)

DfES = Department for Educational and Skills (**www.dfes.gov.uk**)

The Government will have invested £459 million between 2003/04 and 2005/06 in support of the project. The objective of this initiative is to enhance the take-up of sport by school children in England who currently spend a minimum of two hours each week on high quality PE and school sport.

The initiative has eight sub-delivery areas that are identified in a Government document called *Learning through Sport*.

Toolkit: Delivery area objectives

The table below identifies some of the delivery areas. Research the objectives of each of these delivery areas.

Delivery areas	Objectives
Specialist Sports Colleges	e.g. *To spread best practice and raise standards in sport*
Sports 'Academies'	
School Sports Co-ordinators	
Step into Sport	
School/Club Links	

Tutor talk

As a Community Sports Development Officer you need to be aware of how these initiatives are impacting on your local area and your own sports. With guidance from your tutor research and review what initiatives have been implemented in your locality and produce a short report on one of these initiatives.

Who's in charge?

Most sports have international and national, autonomous governing bodies that are responsible for the organisation and structure of that particular sport. There are some governing bodies that are really well known. For example, the governing body of football is the **Football Association** (the FA); the governing body of rugby is the **Rugby Football Union** (the RFU). However, there are others that are less well known unless you are involved in that sport. For example, the Welsh Handball Association, which differs from the British Handball Association.

All these governing bodies have emerged over the last 150 years from the need to have some standardisation and harmonisation within their sport. Many of these governing bodies originally had strong ties to the middle and upper classes of the 19th century and in some cases elements of these links still exist today. It was only in 1995 that Will Carling made reference to the "59 farts that ran the Rugby Football Union". The diagram below illustrates how your club(s) fit into the national and international structure and organisation of your sport.

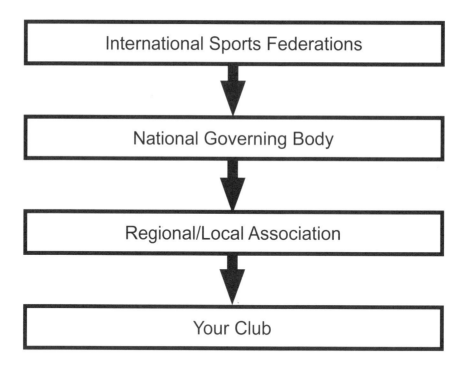

Today, many governing bodies are no longer reliant on the voluntary contributions of enthusiastic amateurs, but have in place a professional organisational structure that can support the increasing range of roles and responsibilities they undertake. Although each governing body is independent, their mouthpiece is the **Central Council of Physical Recreation**, which acts as the voice of over 240 governing bodies to both the Government and Sport England. Whether you play recreational sport or play at a high level you will be directly affected by the decisions and activities of your governing bodies.

Toolkit: Researching your governing bodies' roles and responsibilities

Research the major roles and responsibilities of your governing body and give specific recent examples.

Roles and responsibilities	Examples
To organise competitions and leagues	

Author's advice

Later on in the book you are to investigate two sports that are important in your own area. So you might like to use either of these sports to investigate a governing body. If you are not sure who is the governing body of sport, a good source of information would be the *Encyclopaedia of British Sport*. Another good starting point here would be to access the Sport England website, which you should now familiar with. Once you have identified your national governing body either write to them for information or alternatively use their website. Again, spend some time exploring this as later you will need to refer to it again.

In the main body of the report you are to produce at the end of *Section 2*, you have to explore the development and organisation of the sports industry. You will have to include a historical perspective through the sports you have chosen to research. This will be an important element of your **IVA**. A useful way to do this is to produce some visual presentation material for the report.

Toolkit: Sports history exhibition called 'Then & Now'

You are to develop a visual presentation of the historical development of a sport that has its roots in 19th century England or earlier and contrast it with today. Identify any social changes that led to changes in the sport during the 20th century. Look at main groups involved, the kit they played in, the equipment they used and the important changes that took place.

Create a wall display of a timeline of your chosen sports identifying important dates and events in their development.

 Author's advice

Try to gather as much visual material as you can to complete this. Good sources of information are the sport studies text books and specialist sports history books as well as the Internet. Your local museum service might be helpful in finding other sources.

A timeline is a simple way of presenting the historical development of your sports in time or chronological order. (You have already seen a simple example of one for the PE syllabi.) You could include pictures or diagrams here that you come across that give a feel for each period you identify.

A useful website providing information and links on the history of sport can be found here: http://www2.umist.ac.uk/sport/sports history/index2.html.

Toolkit: Role, structure and functions of the governing bodies

You are to undertake some research about the role, structure and functions of the governing body of a sport that you are involved in or wish to research about.

Fill in the chart below:

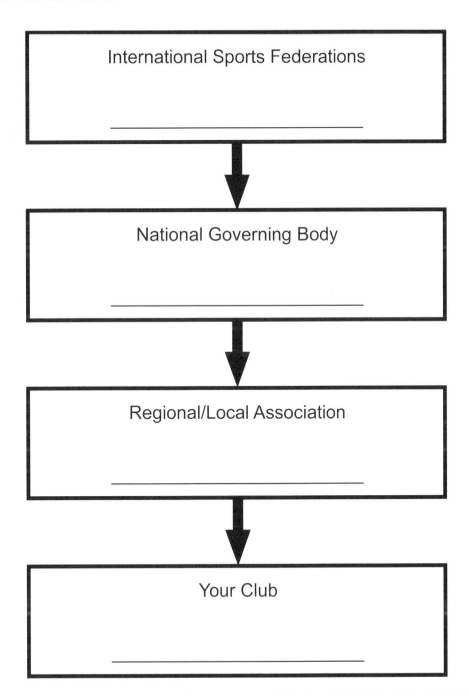

International Sports Federations

_____

National Governing Body

_____

Regional/Local Association

_____

Your Club

_____

Section 2: Is size important?

LO1:   Review the development and changing nature of sport

LO3:   Investigate the scale of the sports industry

Section 2 continues to examine the changing nature of sport and the developing scale of the sports industry. This will include information relating to Learning Outcome 3 but will also cover further elements of Learning Outcome 1.

As an introduction to your final report you will need to explain the current scale and economic importance of the sports industry with particular reference to two sports you will chose for a more detailed investigation. These two sports will be the focus of your research.

You will constantly read about reference to the **sports industry**. What does this mean? By now you should be fairly clear about what sport involves. It involves such characteristics as physical activity, rules, enjoyable, and competitive with some element of chance.

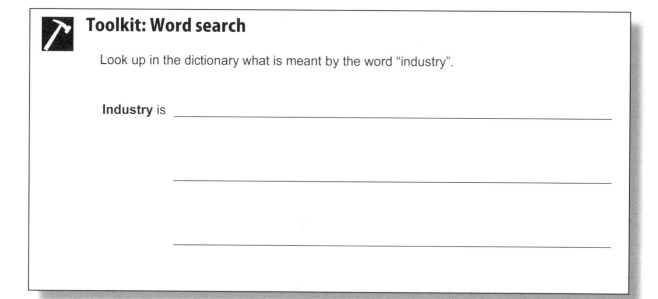

Toolkit: Word search

Look up in the dictionary what is meant by the word "industry".

Industry is _____

_____

_____

Author's advice

Try to be clear on what makes it an industry rather than just games/sports that can be played. It includes a vast range of activities, each of which has a different purpose. For example, does it involve making money? If so, how?

Toolkit: Reasons why the sports industry is important

Individually or in groups draw up reasons why the sports industry is important.

Reasons	Local examples
Employment	A number of retail sports shops in the area.

Author's advice

From the above exercise you may well have come up with reasons that link to the number of people who play the sports, the range and variety of jobs that the sports create or the amount of money that it generates.

Toolkit: Definitions

Complete the following definitions:

1. The number of people who play the sport.

This is called P__ __ __ __ __ __ __ __ __ __

2. The number of people who work in the industry.

This is called E __ __ __ __ __ __ __ __ __

3. The amount of money it makes.

Often referred to as R __ __ __ __ __ __ or financial turnover

Toolkit: Sports industry parts spider-gram

Draw up a spider-gram of the all the different parts of the sports industry.

Components of sport

Retail sport (e.g. JJB, Intersport etc.)

Employment

The sports industry is a growth sector for employment in which there is a need for staff with up-to-date and flexible skills. At present there are over 621,000 jobs in paid employment in the sport and recreation industry (*source:* **www.skillsactive.org.uk**) with a projected growth to 750,000 by 2008. It is not only the number of jobs, but also the wide range of employment opportunities in sport that is important. These may range from coaching, to playing professionally to administrating.

 Toolkit: Researching job opportunities

Research the range of job opportunities that link into the two sports of your choice. When you research employment opportunities remember in this case you are researching paid employment and not voluntary employment. Also remember some jobs are not directly related to playing the sport, e.g. a physiotherapist might be employed by either a club or a facility. Useful sources of information here will be **Skills Active** (**www.skillsactive.org.uk**) which is the industry sector Skills Council and is responsible for skills training within the industry.

For example:

Sport: *Netball*	Sport: *Swimming*
Regional Sports Development Officer	*Club coach*

Sport:	Sport:

Size of the industry

The economic scale of the sports industry is quite a significant factor in our national economy. Apart from the number of jobs within this industry, the latest figures illustrate that sport generated £9.8bn and that sport-related employment provides households in England with £5.8bn in disposable income. Most of the sport-related income comes from the private sector. Sport contributes £5.5bn to central government through taxes and people in England spend £2.7bn each year participating in sport (*The Value of the Sports Economy in England in 2000*). There are over 231,000 businesses and organisations throughout the UK spread amongst the public, private and voluntary sector.

Toolkit: Profiles of companies or organisations in sport

Produce a profile of two companies or organisations involved in either the **Sport and Recreation** or **Health and Fitness** sectors of the sports industry. One should be a local company, the other a national company. The profile should include:

- name of company
- marketing material
- range of activities undertaken
- number of sites
- years established
- number of people employed by the company or organisation
- if possible, the annual turnover.

Author's advice

It is unlikely that a local private company will release financial information to you. However, Public Limited Companies have to publish their accounts and both Local Authority organisation accounts and Voluntary Organisation accounts should be available to you.

Participation

Size and scale of the industry is dependent on the number of people who are participating either as players or as spectators, or consumers of the goods and services on offer.

Toolkit: Researching national participation of sports

Research the annual national participation rates for your two sports for the past ten years. Put your result in the form of a graph to identify whether the trend of participation is upwards or downwards.

Author's advice

Write to the governing body to obtain information from them or alternatively use their website. Other useful sources of information would be the General Household Survey and Social Trends, Key Note, Mintel….the list goes on. Speak to your librarian for help, guidance, advice and support in researching facts and statistics on the Internet and from publications your library may stock. Find out whether participation rates, that is the number of people taking part on a regular basis, in your sports are increasing or decreasing over a period of time.

Sectors – who provides what?

There are many different components that make up the industry. These include a range of different sport and recreational activities, the health and fitness sector and the outdoor sector. Some are concerned with playing different sports either recreationally or professional, some to do with providing equipment, some relate to improving our health and fitness. The **sports industry** covers such a wide range of activities that are provided for by different individuals, groups or organisations. The diagram below divides the industry into different sectors of providers.

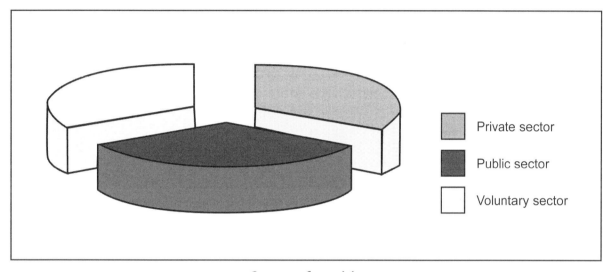

■ Private sector

■ Public sector

□ Voluntary sector

Sectors of provision

A sector refers to a slice of the providers that have the same general aims and objectives. For example, you or a member of your family may belong to a private gym owned either by an individual or a company who want to make a profit from that business. You may also play for a local sports club run by a group of enthusiastic volunteers who give of their time freely and who are not interested in making a profit. You may also use a facility such as a swimming pool that is provided for you as a service by the local authority where you live.

Toolkit: Examining the private, public, and voluntary sectors

1. Read the following statements and identify which sector they describe:

- Sport and leisure activities, services and facilities are organised by local authorities and are available to everyone in the community. This sector is mainly funded by local taxation and funding.

This is known as the _____ Sector

- Provides a service to the local population but provides the facilities, activities and programmes in order to make a financial profit.

This is known as the _____ Sector

- This is the biggest sector and is made up of a mix of small, medium and large organisations which support communities, groups and sports on a non profit making basis.

This is known as the _____ Sector

2. Complete the table of all of the sports and physical recreational activities in which you and your family participate. Identify where these are undertaken, who provides them and which sector they fall into.

Activities/sports	Facilities	Provider	Sector

Author's advice

One of your tasks as a Community Sports Development Officer is to build up a database or directory of sports providers, facilities, and funding agencies. It will be easier for you to start this process straight away, so design a database using an IT software programme such as Microsoft Excel or Access.

Once you have created this database, it is worthwhile keeping the information. You may need to contact the people and organisations again in the future and it will save you time and effort in finding it again.

As you should know by now, for any sport to be important means that it contributes to the local economy and social life of that community through consumer spending, revenue generation, providing employment opportunities or because there is a high participation rate.

A good starting point for assessing the importance of particular sports is to look at the coverage they are given in the local paper.

 Toolkit: Importance of local sports industries

From the table of sports you have identified pick out the two sports that you think are important parts of the sports industry where you live and write a short introduction as to why they are important.

Sport	Reasons of importance in your region	Local examples
	1. 2. 3.	
	1. 2. 3.	

Author's advice

You will need to research the size and scale of the industry in relation to the two sports of your choice and these factors will be important. Here you need to think back to the activity where you identified factors that included **participation rates**, **employment opportunities** and **revenue generation**.

A very useful source of information about the scale, and economic impact of sport can be found in a national study that Sport England has recently published called *Value of Sport and the Economy*. There are also regional reports that specifically feature information on your locality. These can be found at **www.sportengland.org**. Also refer to the Skills Active site **www.skillsactive.org.uk**.

Toolkit: Identifying your local sports providers

Identify the main providers for your chosen sports. Write to the mangers of facilities or administrators of the sports you have chosen and arrange an interview with them.

Prepare a short set of questions before you go. You want to find out:

- What sector are they in?
- What do they offer?
- What are their main sources/streams of income?
- What do they think is the main image of their sector is?
- Do they work in partnership with other sectors?

Complete and if possible record your interviews using a tape recorder.

Collect samples of their publicity materials.

Prepare a short presentation that you would be able to give to either your tutor or your class group.

Author's advice

Select sports that you are interested in or in which you participate and involve different sector providers. For example, if you use a gym, select Health and Fitness. This could be provided by both the private and public sectors. If you play for a basketball team at a local sports centre, this could involve the public sector and voluntary sector.

Funding – money ··· money ··· money

To be involved in sport in any capacity will cost money. The funding of sports is therefore very important. It is important that in your role as a Community Sports Development Officer that you can identify major sources of funding and how these can be accessed. This might mean advising on the availability of grants or helping to find different sources of sponsorship for an activity or an individual.

Sometimes it is difficult to appreciate how expensive it can be to be involved in sport. For some people the cost might be prohibitive.

 Toolkit: How much it costs to participate in sport

Draw up an annual account of how much it costs you to participate in your sport. Start by drawing up a list of the costs involved in playing or supporting your local team. These might include equipment costs, transportation costs, coaching and playing costs and social costs.

Use a spreadsheet software package to do this such as Microsoft Excel. Some of your data will be guesstimates, but try to be as accurate as you can.

What you will appreciate through this exercise is that involvement in sports can be expensive and needs to be paid for. You as an individual may have different sources of funding to be able to participate. For example, you may have a part-time job or you may receive financial support from your parents. You might at particular times have applied for a grant to assist you.

Your sports will have different sources of funding. These might include such sources as membership fees, grants, loans, sponsorship deals and possibly, if important enough, a television deal.

Toolkit: Investigating sources and amounts of funding

Review the latest annual reports for your sports and draw up a table that identifies the various sources of funding and the amount they received.

You should have begun to appreciate that there is a range of different sources or streams of funding available for sport. So let's begin to research how your sports are funded. It would be useful for you to research the governing bodies of your sport, your local authority, Sports England and the DCMS to help you identify sources of funding. Each governing body has to publish its annual accounts in its annual report.

Name of sport (1):

Types of funding	The amount
e.g. Sponsorship deals	£
	£
	£
	£
	£

Name of sport (2):

Types of funding	The amount
e.g. Subscription fees	£
	£
	£
	£
	£

Sponsorship

Sponsorship comes in many guises. It might be a local business supporting a local league team through providing shirts; it might be a local company that puts its name to a local league or competition; it might be a national company that sponsors a national event; or it might be a multinational company that sees value in supporting the activities of particular elite athletes or particular international events such as the World Cup or the Olympic Games.

Toolkit: Definition of sponsorship

Complete the following definition:

Sponsorship is _____

_____

Sponsorship is a major source of income and many sports now rely on sponsorship deals at both national and local level. There is now an Institute of Sports Sponsorship, **www.sports-sponsorship.co.uk**. Organisations and individuals become involved in sponsorship for a number of reasons, but it does involve a relationship between the sponsor and the sport. Businesses that are involved as sponsors in the UK now invest more than £1bn annually in sport.

Toolkit: Sponsorship activities

The activities involved are as varied and innovative as the imaginations of the participants. List as many different types of sponsorship activities as you can.

Types of activities	Examples
Sponsorship of a football club	Manchester United and Nike

Toolkit: Sponsorship at local and international levels

Take your chosen sports and research sponsorship deals within these levels:

1. At a local level.

This might just involve a local trader supporting your local club. Go and talk to them about their reasons for doing this.

Questions you might like to consider are:

*   What the sponsorship involves?

*   What it costs?

*   What he/she hopes to get from it?

*   What the benefits for the club are?

2. At a national level.

Then research if your governing body has negotiated any major sponsorship deals and what they involve.

Questions to consider here are:

*   Is it at elite or grassroots level?

*   How much is the sponsorship worth?

*   What is the purpose of the sponsorship?

*   How is the money spent?

*   What does the organisation gain from the sponsorship?

*   How does it benefit the sport?

The role of the media

There is a direct link between funding of particular sports and the **media**. As you already appreciate sport has become increasingly commercialised. The role of the media has been closely linked to this process of commercialisation and there is a very close relationship between some sports and the media in which both parties benefit. Sports relationship with the media has been very important in the growth and popularity of some of our major sports. **Television** companies in particular are prepared to pay a great deal of money to cover particular sports. For example, BSkyB TV has for the past decade negotiated a deal with the Premier League for TV rights to their games worth millions of pounds. American TV companies pay hundreds of millions of dollars for the exclusive rights to the Olympics. In 1960 they paid $400,000 for the TV rights for the Rome Olympics. Forty years later they paid $705,000,000 for the rights to the 2000 Sydney Olympics. Media coverage and, in particular, TV media coverage brings in sponsorship and money to these sports.

Toolkit: Research a rights deal

Research a major television or newspaper rights deal that has been important for the growth and development of a particular sport.

When you refer to the media say what you mean because the media covers a range of activities and it provides coverage in different ways.

The relationship between sport and the media is a symbiotic relationship (this means there are benefits to both sides). Whilst it may be obvious that media coverage provides benefits for a sport, e.g. increased exposure or increased revenue, the benefits to the media of this coverage are not so obvious.

Toolkit: Sources and characteristics of media coverage

Identify different sources of media coverage and their main characteristics.

Media source	Main characteristics
Television	Visual Instant Action

Toolkit: The importance of media cover

List five reasons why you think sport is an important part of media coverage.

1. _____

2. _____

3. _____

4. _____

5. _____

The different kinds of media exposure have had a massive influence on the way that different sports are developing. For example, we have seen the introduction of new rules to make games more exciting, we have seen the use of media technology to help officials make decisions and we have seen the development of new versions of traditional sports to make them more marketable, e.g. 20-20 cricket. In the next activity you are to think about ways in which the media has changed your sports.

Toolkit: Media impact on sport

Identify ways in which the media has impacted on the sports of your choice.

1. _____

2. _____

3. _____

4. _____

Of course the media does not provide comprehensive coverage of all sports and it seems that only a few sports benefit from media exposure. So what makes a sport attractive to particular types of media?

Toolkit: Study two types of media coverage

Over the next week make a detailed study of two types of media coverage from your own list.

In the table below:

- Identify the types of sports they covered in this period.
- Identify the amount of time/space they have given over to each sport.
- Give reasons for these choices.

Types of sports	Time/space	Reasons why

Image and the media – I'd better look good because I am on telly

This symbiotic relationship between sport and the media is not just economic. You need to be aware of the power of the media and the way it can impact either negatively or positively on your chosen sports or players within those sports. The reason the term media is used is because sports are mediated or represented to readers, listeners and viewers through selected images or messages. For example, you might have been to watch a match live and then later watched edited highlights of the same match. Sometimes you might have wondered if it is the same match because the editor has selected parts of the match to make it more exciting and worth watching. What you see is someone else's representation of what is happening.

You need to think about how the media portrays your sport. Important questions are:

- How is the sport presented?

- What sort of images or messages are portrayed?

- What effect does it have upon our behaviours, e.g. gambling, imitation of role models, participation, competitiveness?

- How is the sport presented negatively through media exposure?

- How is the sport presented positively?

- How does it reinforce particular themes, e.g. the role of women in sport, excessive nationalism, race, and multi national companies?

 ### Toolkit: Sport in the news

Review a tabloid newspaper for the next week.

Analyse the content of coverage given over to sport or sports people.

Consider the amount of coverage, (as indicated by the number of articles, photographs and column inches devoted to each of the following categories:

- age – U12s, adolescents, young adults, middle aged and older persons
- race – ethnic minorities
- gender – male and female
- physical status – able bodied or disabled.

Consider the nature of the coverage:

Note the articles and pictures emphasise, e.g.:

- performance and skill levels
- appearance of the athlete
- sensationalises lifestyles of famous sports people
- intensity of involvement

- sports personalities
- nationalistic aspects of sport
- negative or positive images of sport.

Author's advice

Do not just look in the sports section but also in other parts of the paper. Devise some way of quantifying this information (e.g. number of pages, number of pictures, size and location of articles – front page, etc). You could use a table format or create charts that indicate the emphasis adopted by the press. Also cut out some articles or pictures that provide good examples of this emphasis.

Toolkit: Sport in the news (continued)

Finally, draw up two lists:

1. List the positive or good impacts of the media.
2. List the negative or bad impacts of the media.

Positive impacts	Negative impacts

An important area that will help to attract income to sport is the development of new technology. New media technology, and in particular development of the Internet, are already changing media exposure of sport and having a significant impact on both its commercial potential and how it is presented. You need to think through how this change has – and will in the future – impact on your own sports and the sports industry in general.

Toolkit: Positive image of sport presentation

Using the research you have already undertaken on the media, prepare a presentation that explains the role of the media in presenting a positive image of your two chosen sports.

You need to explain how the media can be a two-edged sword and can project both negative and positive images. It should include comparisons of different types of media and how they project a sport. Finally, you need suggest what needs to be done to improve media impact in the future.

Author's advice

This activity will help you prepare you a significant element of your **IVA**. It is important that you feel confident about giving such a presentation. You might wish to utilise PowerPoint software to assist you with the presentation. You will gain confidence by practising and rehearsing it carefully. It is useful to prepare some prompt notes to remind you what you want to say and that these link to the media presentation. Do not just repeat what you have included in the media presentation. Ask a couple of friends or relatives to listen to what you want to say and watch your presentation. Ask for comments.

You should now be ready for the presentation. Good luck!

Grants and loans – how can I find some money?

Sponsorship and media rights income is not the only source of income for sport. Indeed most sports find it very difficult to generate sponsorship and must search for other sources. The Government is investing large amounts of money into school and community sports facilities; particular projects include the **New Opportunities Fund's** school sport programme, the **PE School Sport and Club Links Programme**, **Active England** and the **Community Club Development Programme**. The local authority sports sector received about £740m in sports-related grants from central government, which represents about £15 per person. Whilst there is very little data about the voluntary sector, it is estimated that the combined income for this sector is £3.3bn of which only 1/3 comes from subscriptions.

An important source of funding has been the awards of loans and grants to particular sports or groups. These can be given by a local **Sports Council**, **Sports Federation**, **Sports Alliance**, the local authority or by national government.

A very important source of grant provision over the last decade has been the **National Lottery**.

Author's advice

You should by now be familiar with using the Internet to research such questions. A useful start in identifying sources of information to answer these questions is the **National Lottery Commission** website: **www.natlotcomm.gov.uk**. Remember to keep a record of the different sources of information for your bibliography.

Toolkit: Facts about the National Lottery

Answer the following questions about the National Lottery:

1. Who organises and runs the National Lottery?
2. The National Lottery works in partnership with a number of lottery distributors, to support good causes in the arts, sports, heritage, health, education, environment, community and charity sectors. Which distributor is responsible for sport?
3. What is the Community Projects Capital Fund?
4. Who does the Active Communities Development Fund target and what is the maximum that can be given annually?
5. What National Lottery sponsored programme supports elite athletes to compete in their sport and who administers this?

 Toolkit: The National Lottery in action

Describe one lottery award within your locality.

 Author's advice

This task is designed for you to do some research on local lottery awards that have impacted on one or more of your selected sports. There is a **National Lottery Awards Search Database** (**www.lottery.culture.gov.uk/introduction.asp**) that will provide you with a starting point to identify awards that have allocated within your own areas. If possible, link this to one of your chosen sports.

Both *Section 1* and *Section 2* has been concerned with identifying the development, changing nature of sport and the growth of the sports industry as a significant part of the national economy. In these sections you have researched and looked at how sports are organised, the role of education, possible sources of funding and the influence of the media on its development.

Assessment activity (IVA) 1

LO1   Review the development and changing nature of sport

LO3   Investigate the scale of the sports industry

In this final exercise you are to prepare a report for local clubs on the sports industry, both locally and nationally. The focus of this report will be your two selected sports.

1. In the introduction to your report, explain the current size and economic importance of the sports industry with reference to the sports of your choice in relation to employment, participation and financial turnover.

2. In the main body of the report, explore the development and organisation of the sports industry today. This is to include: historical development of sport and the role of education in that development; the organisation of sport through the different sectors; how your sports are funded, both historically and currently; and the impact of the media and sponsorship using your sports as case studies.

3. In the final part of this section, provide a summary of your findings in the two sports of your choice, draw some conclusions and critically evaluate how important the different factors are.

 Author's advice

This activity is the culmination of the research and activities you have undertaken in sections 1 and 2 and will provide you with evidence for coverage of two of your main learning outcomes and links into one of your main tasks for the IVA. It is important that you are able:

- to summarise your findings
- draw conclusions from these
- critically evaluate these conclusions.

Toolkit: Defining summary, conclusions and critical evaluation

Look at the following three statements and identify them as either:

Summary   Conclusions   Critical evaluation

- 'Final opinion or statement(s) of the logical result' = _____

- 'Dispensing with details or brief account' = _____

- 'Give a reasoned positive or negative value to' = _____

Use a dictionary check whether your understanding is correct.

The diagram below identifies the different stages you need to go through to be able to critically evaluate. You need to know what each stage involves. The final activity is to help you understand what is required.

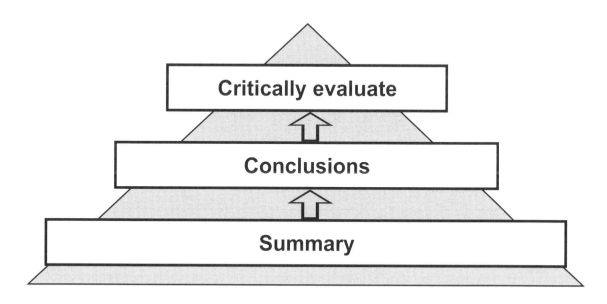

The stages of critical evaluation

Toolkit: Critical evaluation of your work

1.   Summary

Read through your work and summarise in bullet form the main findings. For example:

- Two important sports/recreational activities are football and Health/Fitness through gym memberships.

- Number of Gyms are XX.

2.   Conclusions

Review your findings and summary carefully. Draw up your final conclusions/opinions on these in bullet points.

Put these conclusions into rank order, i.e. those you consider the most important first (often referred to as significant).

Explain your reason for each bullet and why?

3.   Critical evaluation

Use the table below to help you order your thinking.

Rank	Bullet points	Reasons

When you have gone through this process, you are ready to write up your report.

You should now be familiar with both the **DCMS** and **Sport England** websites. Go back to them and review how they have structured sports reports.

Structuring your report

A written report is a document that provides an account of your investigations. They should be structured documents which contain discrete sections and subheadings within each section. You should structure the report to the following format:

1. **A title page** showing the title of the report, the author's name and date of publication.

2. **A contents page** detailing all sections of the report and subsections with page numbers.

3. **A summary** of your main findings.

4. **An introduction** to include:

    *   terms of reference

    *   how you obtained your information

    *   topics covered.

5. **Main content** of the report: broken down into sections and subsections.

6. **Conclusions** indicating what the report has found

7. **Recommendations for further actions.**

8. **Appendices.**

9. **Bibliography** providing information sources, books, websites and magazines. Give authors, date and title of publication, publisher and, if appropriate, page numbers.

Section 3: How much choice do I have?

LO2:　Explore the social influences on sports participation

Author's advice

Much of what you do in this section links into the work you will require for the ethics and values module and that part of the IVA.

Reasons for participation – why do we do it?

It has already been identified that sports are **socially constructed** by different **socio-economic groups** and **interest groups** interacting with each other.

Sporting activities do not just appear. They are the result of people and groups meeting, interacting and socialising in particular ways. They have emerged, changed and continue to change as a result of those interactions. People must think they are important and value what sports offer them as individuals and offers the community or society in which they live. It could be something as simple as the opportunity to meet other like-minded people or to get fit. It could also offer excitement in an otherwise boring existence. At a societal level, sports activities can be used by governments, local authorities to counter antisocial behaviour from particular groups at risk, or improve the health of the nation or generate a sense of pride within the country.

Toolkit

Individually or as part of a group identify the benefits that sport provides both for the individual and society. To start this exercise fill the blanks below:

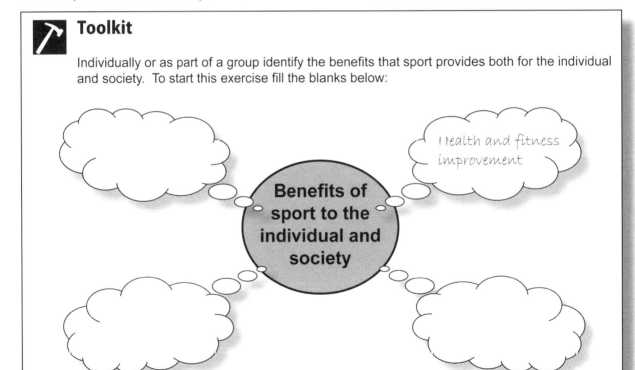

The reasons why we take part in physical activity and sports are very complex. From the above exercise you may well have come up with a wide range of reasons as to why it is important to participate and why we should all be involved in some form of physical activity if not in sport itself. These might include the opportunity to socialise with other people, as a stress reliever, as part of a healthy lifestyle, the need for some physical exercise in an increasingly sedentary lifestyle, to experience some excitement or a mix of all of these.

Wiggins et al, 2000 suggest there is a need for a co-ordinated equitable approach to the provision of sporting opportunities that should address two main areas. One is sports equity, which we shall examine later, the other is sports development. This enables people to learn basic skills with the possibility of reaching an elite standard of excellence. Sport England has produced a sports development model based on a pyramid of participation and development.

Sports development model

Elite sport
International competition
Olympic Games,
World championships, etc

Performance
National competitions and squads

Performance
Coaching, competition and training
Local and regional competitions

Participation
Exercising for a variety of reasons
Health, fitness, social reasons

Foundation level
Learning basic movement skills, knowledge and developing
a positive attitude to physical activity
Primary school age

Toolkit: How lifestyle changes have affected sport

Interview some one who was your age in the 1950s' and ask them some questions about their lifestyle at that time. Some of the things you might like to think about are:

- Did they have a job and if so what was it?
- Did they own a car?
- What was they main form of transportation?
- What kind of diet did they have?
- What sort of physical leisure/sport activities did they do?
- How much money did they have to spend on leisure pursuits?
- What sort of holidays did they take and how many a year?
- What sort of exercise did they take and how often?
- Were they a member of a gym?
- Why did they participate in these physical activities?

Compare this with your lifestyle today and draw up list of similarities and differences.

Similarities	Differences

Toolkit: Local and regional sports development

Using the sports development model on page 55, fill in what is happening locally and regionally in your areas for the two sports of your choice.

Elite sport – to be the best or just to take part

There has been significant investment in elite sport and its use in promoting our country as a successful, energetic society. It can also bring us together and provide a sense of unity. Think back to previous World Cups or Olympic Games and the sense of pride that is generated by the success of our teams or individual athletes, e.g. Kelly Holmes.

In 1996, under John Major's Government, UK Sport was established by **Royal Charter** to drive the development of world-class, high performance in the UK. It is responsible for the management and distribution of £29 million annually and it distributes 9.2% of the **National Lottery** sport allocation towards the development of excellence in world terms.

Toolkit: Investigating UK Sport

Go to the UK website **www.uksport.gov.uk** and complete the following tasks:

- Identify the main goals of UK Sport.
- Identify other agencies it works with.
- Identify those groups of athletics it supports.
- Find out the aims of the world-class performance programme and how these are met.

Health and fitness

This great investment in sport is not just about finding the next Kelly Holmes or David Beckham. It is considered important because sport and PE is a vehicle that has the potential to introduce young people – from as early as four years old – to the benefits of an active and healthy lifestyle. This is not something new. Since as early as the development of the 1902 PE syllabus, there has been general concern about the fitness levels of people in general and the young in particular. However, as you are probably aware, your present lifestyle is becoming less physically active and more sedentary than perhaps that of your parents or grandparents.

The Government is becoming increasingly concerned about the present state of the health of the nation. One such initiative promoted by DCMS is the **healthy living blueprint for schools**. This pulls together the Government's advice on healthy eating and lifestyles for schools. The aim is to give children the knowledge, skills and understanding they need to lead healthy lives, not just through what is taught, but also through the school's curriculum organisation and environment

The main objectives of the **healthy living blueprint for schools** are:

- promoting a school environment which encourages a proactive approach to developing a healthy lifestyle
- using the curriculum to teach about healthy lifestyles
- ensuring healthy food and drink choices are available throughout the school day
- providing high quality physical education and school sports
- promoting an understanding of lifelong health through personal, social and health education (PSHE).

There has also been an increasing recognition within the medical professions of the importance of exercise and a healthy diet in treating a range of different medical conditions: heart conditions, obesity, diabetes and some cancers are just some examples. Many local health centres now run or promote exercise referral schemes either within the centre itself or in partnership with local gymnasiums or leisure centres.

Toolkit: Researching exercise referral schemes

Go to your local health centre and enquire whether they are running an exercise referral scheme. If they are, research the following:

- How long has the scheme been running?
- What is the aim of the scheme?
- Who is responsible for it?
- How is progress monitored?
- Which conditions does it target?
- How successful has it been?

Author's advice

The medical personnel at health centres are very busy. You will need to make an appointment to speak with someone about the scheme. Remember also there are issues around confidentiality, so make sure the questions you ask are very general ones and not specific to individual cases. The centre may also have a leaflet about its scheme and this may give you the information you need.

There has also been over the past decade a massive growth in the development of the health and fitness industry driven by an increasing awareness of health and exercise issues and the commercial exploitation of this by the private sector. This growth includes proliferation of local gyms, development of a range of therapy activities such as aromatherapy, sports therapy, health food stores and exercise referral schemes from health centres.

 Toolkit

Create a database of health-related activities and facilities in your local region that includes what it is, where it is and who to contact.

No person is an island

While individual lifestyle decisions (such as diet and exercise) will have an important effect, there are many other factors that lie outside of an individual's control but that can still directly influence their health. Factors such as: poverty, social exclusion, employment, housing, education and the environment are all important. You now need to investigate how some of these social factors influence what different groups and individuals can do and what they cannot do. As a Community Sports Development officer you may be required to provide local clubs or groups with advice and guidance on how to increase participation in their activities.

What is meant by social influences?

If you can remember back to one of your early exercises, you were asked about what society "means". Whilst there are different types of society, there are certain common features, e.g. people interact with each other and depend on each other. There are certain written and unwritten rules by which society functions. No one person is an island and no one can live completely independently and therefore each of you is going to be influenced by others within that society. So people exist **interdependently**.

In stating the obvious that sport activities are social activities this does not mean only that you socialise in meeting and playing with friends. It also means there are a number of other social links. For example, where you are born, brought up, who your parents are and which school you went to are some of the social influences that will determine the type of sports activities you participate in.

Toolkit: Mapping social influences on your sporting interests

Do this in the form of a spider-gram to enable you to trace clearly the different influences.

Use the diagram below:

Toolkit: Categorising the social influences of your sporting interests

Individually or in groups see if you can put the influences you have identified under some general headings, e.g.:

- How much money is available?
- Types of jobs you or your parents have?
- Where you go to school?
- What country you are from?

- What part of the country you live?
- What facilities are available
- What ethnic group you are from?
- Not being allowed to play a sport because it is not considered suitable?

When you have completed this, discuss within your group which of the headings below fit your own classification.

Insert these in the table below:

Cultural influences/ ethnic background	Gender and stereotyping	Income and socio-economic status	Accessibility/ opportunity factors

The above categories have been identified as important social influences. There are certain groups of people though who for various social reasons do not seem to have the same opportunities to participate in sport. Achieving equality of opportunity (also referred to as equity) in sport involves:

- recognising certain groups are disadvantaged
- treating everyone equally, but recognising that some groups of people have different needs
- making sport accessible to all.

Social class and economic status (socio-economic groupings)

Social class is difficult to define but it is a way of grouping people together or classifying them based on common social features. It will be useful for you to think about the different characteristics that make up a social grouping or class. Working class, middle class and upper class have been traditional labels used to classify the different social groupings. However, it is far more complex than this and has different dimensions, ranging from the type of job a person does to the amount of time a person has for their leisure activities and to the type of leisure activities they are involved with.

 Toolkit: Characteristics of social class

List as many characteristics of social class as you can:

1. e.g. *Area where I live*

2. _____

3. _____

4. _____

5. _____

6. _____

In all social research, occupation is identified as the main determinant of social class. Hence the term **socio-economic status** is used.

 Toolkit: Researching government surveys

Research a government survey, e.g. *General Household Survey* or *Social Trends* and identify the categories of classification. Next, carry out the following:

1. Identify which socio-economic group you belong to.
2. Identify if there is any relationship between socio-economic status and participation rates in sport.
3. Research through these surveys or other databases whether there is a link between socio-economic groupings and participation in your own sports.

 Author's advice

You are looking to see if there is a relationship between the two factors: socio-economic group and participation. Try to represent the relationship in a visual format. Think about what would be the best form of presentation that clearly illustrates the relationship, e.g. bar chart, pie chart or graph.

The statistical data produced by surveys such as the *General Household Survey* or *Social Trends* gives little explanation of how your socio-economic status might either allow you or prevent you from doing activities you might wish to do. *Hayward, 1989*, suggests that there are two dimensions to understanding how social classification impacts on leisure choices:

1. An objective dimension, which relates to your position in the labour market, the type and amount of education you have, the income you earn and the area where you live.

2. A subjective dimension, which is less measurable but relates to imagery about particular groups based upon their accents, the way they speak how they dress, social networks, car ownership and the leisure activities.

There is some evidence to suggest that higher socio-economic groups enjoy a more varied and more active range of leisure activities. There is also some evidence that relates the type of sports and activities with particular social groupings.

 Toolkit: Identifying class connotations

Either individually or as a group, identify the class connotations of the following activities:

- greyhound racing
- fly-fishing
- fox hunting
- darts
- hockey
- tennis
- boxing
- soccer
- rowing
- weight lifting
- horse racing.

Choose one of the above activities and illustrate how class distinctions are apparent.

Sport for all?

Income and economic status is a major determinant of social class. We are one of the wealthiest societies in the world and this has been a major factor in the development of the sports industry. However, this new wealth has not benefited all groups and has therefore excluded them from access to sport, e.g., ethnic minority groups, young mothers, unemployed and the disabled. People who have low incomes or rely on the State through the benefits system are clearly restricted by the amount of disposable income available for sporting activities. Such groups are often targeted by both the voluntary sector and public sector providers for special consideration. However, sometimes such schemes are counter-productive as these groups do not want to be labelled or stigmatised.

Toolkit: Researching schemes for the unemployed

Research information on a local scheme where you live that target the unemployed to involve them in sport.

Identify:

- the name and objectives of the scheme
- when it is run
- who runs it
- how successful it has been.

Gender

One of the most important relationships between individuals in any society is based on gender and many surveys in Britain indicate that gender is a crucial factor in determining sporting choices and opportunities. Women, for a variety of reasons, have not always had the same opportunities in sport as their male counterparts. Look back again at your work on the media and see how little exposure women's sport is given compared to men's sport.

To quote from *Critcher and Clark, 1985*:

> *"Women have less leisure time, participate less in most leisure activities and draw on narrower range of leisure options than men. They also spend most of their time around home and family."*

The sex of a person refers to the biological aspect of a person, either male or female; gender roles refer to what different societies and cultures attribute as appropriate behaviour for that sex. These can vary from culture to culture and also change historically within a culture. However, these often lead to **stereotypical views** of what a group can or cannot do.

 Author's advice

You need to be aware that stereotyping is not just unique to women but also impact on other groups such as people with disabilities, young people, and people from different ethnic origins.

Toolkit: Stereotypes

- Research and define the meaning of stereotype.
- What stereotypical views are held in our society about women?
- Examine the two photographs below and discuss which challenges the stereotypical view of women and why?

Author's advice

A very useful source of information on the impact of gender roles on female participation rates is the **Women's Sports Foundation website: www.wsf.org.uk**. Take some time and explore this site.

Sexism is the belief that one sex is inferior to the other and is most often directed towards women. It is sometimes based on the belief that women are not best suited to particular roles in our society. Historically, women have been denied the same political, economic and social rights enjoyed by men based on the myths and stereotypical views you have probably identified. You must not underestimate the effect that these historical attitudes have had on women's opportunities. For example, women continue to be under-represented on the decision-making boards and committees of British sporting bodies and the targets set in the UK strategy for framework for women and sport for 2005 are still not being met.

Toolkit: Sexism in sport questionnaire

Draw up a short questionnaire that you can use to survey your class and other friends.

Find out:

1. which sports they take part in

And

2. how much time they spend doing them.

Analyse your findings as follows:

1. Break down your results into male and female responses.
2. Identify and explain the differences you find.
3. Identify if there are sports that women are excluded from because of their gender and explain the reasons for this.

Quantitative and qualitative questionnaires

Questionnaires are a useful tool to find information about particular groups of people. Questionnaires are not as easily compiled as you might think. First, they must be compatible with the group of people that you are surveying.

When you start to design the questionnaire you need to be clear what your objectives are, i.e. what information do you need to find out.

Questions can be used to gain either **quantitative data**, i.e. data that can be represented numerically

Or

qualitative data, i.e. data that allows respondents to express their views, beliefs, etc, in a non-quantitative manner.

You can include a number of different types of questions.

Closed questions: a number of possible answers are provided and the respondent ticks or circles their answer.

E.g.: Do you participate in sport on a regular basis?   **Yes**   **No**   **Not sure**

However, the above question still leaves some room for improvement. For example, what does regular mean? Sometimes, it is best to ask questions that allow graded or scaled answers.

E.g.: How often do you participate in sport in a week? Less than 1hr   1–3 hrs   4–6 hrs   6+ hrs

Open questions: the respondent is free to answer as he/she wants and is often more appropriate for qualitative data.

E.g.: Why do you think women participate less in sports than men?

Try to keep your questionnaire to one side of A4.

You will find in your school, college or local libraries research method texts that will help you design different types of questions.

On the completion of the questionnaire:

- You need to create a summary sheet for each question and record the responses.

- You then need to present and summarise the data in an appropriate format, e.g. graph or pie charts or perhaps in the form of quotes.

- Finally, you need to draw out the main conclusions from your findings.

There are many different reasons that prevent or discourage women and girls from participating in sport. These include:

Accessibility	Attitudes of others	Commitments
Lack of personal transport	Peer pressure	Work
No public transport	Interests of friends, parents and teachers	Family
No crèche facilities for childcare	Stereotypical views of sports (e.g. women body-builders)	Childcare
High costs of activities	Lack of role models	
Timetable of activities	Lack of confidence	

Toolkit: Promoting sport to males and females

Investigate your chosen sports by visiting at least one facility/centre where they take place to see what is being done to promote those sports for both males and females. Check to see if there are differences in the opportunities that are available to each within the sport and explain why this is happening. Present a short report of your findings to either your tutor or the centre manager.

Cultural influences

Historically, people in all cultures have engaged in different types of playful activities, some of which emerge as sports. However, definitions of sport are influenced by the unique social and cultural characteristics of these societies. If you compare the country you live in to other countries and cultures you will find different types of sporting activities, e.g. whilst American football derives it roots from rugby, it has developed into a separate sport. If you lived in the USA, you would be aware of the importance of sports such as baseball, American football and basketball whilst sports such as football, cricket and rugby are not considered important, major sports. There are many examples of sports that are unique to a country, e.g. hurling in Ireland and pelota in Spain.

Toolkit: Presenting a sport from another country or culture

Research and prepare a presentation on a sport of another country or culture that sounds interesting to you.

The UK is a multicultural society. There will be people within your own class who come from different cultural backgrounds. This not only means that they may originate from different geographical locations, but also have different beliefs, values, foods and traditions that characterise their cultural heritage.

Toolkit: Defining characteristics of cultural groupings

Identify important characteristics that define different cultural groupings.

Cultural differences	Examples
Food	Scottish haggis, kosher meat

Ethnic minority groups

There are many complex definitions which attempt to explain what is meant by an ethnic minority. This simple description may be useful:

"An ethnic minority group is a racial group with a distinct cultural identity, which forms a small percentage of the overall population in a country."

Toolkit: Ethnic minority groupings

1. Individually or through a group discussion draw up a list of ethnic minority groups that are living within your local/regional area.

    Ethnic minority groupings:

    a. _____

    b. _____

    c. _____

    d. _____

2. Select a group from the four you have identified and undertake an investigation of it. Data that might be interesting to find could be as follows:

    Historical data

    *   where the group originated from

    *   when they first arrived in UK.

    Current data

    *   present numbers in the country

    *   present numbers locally

    *   cultural/sports activities specific to the group

    *   religious beliefs.

3. Prepare a feedback session for the class about your ethnic group.

Racism in sport

Racism is still an ethical issue facing sports. The basis of such views emerge from **stereotypical images** that exist about different minority groupings. The myths and beliefs that emerge from such stereotyping limit the opportunities offered and has led to young Afro-Caribbean or Asian athletes being pushed into certain types of sports and even into particular positions within particular sports. Ethnic minority groups are under-represented in position of influence and authority. For example, how many black managers and coaches are there in the English Premier League and does this reflect the number of black players who play in the league?

The friendly international football match between England and Spain in November 2004 brought racism to the forefront again and caused an embarrassment for UEFA and FIFA as well as to the host country. The Spanish minister for sport had to apologise on behalf of the Spanish people for the behaviour of what was a small minority of so-called supporters.

In England, several campaigns have been initiated during the last few years to end racism in sport. Sport England and several NGBs actively promote racial equality in sport.

The public sector has also taken action. In 2001, the **Local Government Association (LGA)**, i.e. the association of all local councils, published *Promoting Racial Equality Through Sport*, a standard for local authority sport and leisure services. The LGA also signed up to the **Charter for Racial Equality in Sport**.

Toolkit: Investigating racism

Before you start on the tasks below, get a dictionary and find out the definition for racism.

Racism is _____

1. From your memory, list racial incidents that have occurred in sport in recent years.
2. Find out about Sport England's policy on racial equality (**www.sportengland.org**).
3. Investigate what anti-racism campaigns are currently held in sport. Try two or three of the larger NGBs.
4. You are the Professional Footballers' Association Chairman. Write a letter to UEFA complaining about racial abuse suffered by black England players during an international football match. In your letter you should:

   • Explain why racism has no place in modern sport and society.

   • Suggest what can be done to stop racism.

   • Explain what racial abuse does for the image of the "abusers" country.

   • Explain what consequences open racial abuse can have for the sport.

   • Demand sanctions should be put in place if racial abuse re-occurs.

People with disabilities

A third important group of people who have experienced barriers to their participation are those who have some form of disability. The 2001 Census data identified that 5% of the population is registered disabled. Disabilities stem from genetic abnormality, disease or accidents and cover a range of sensory, physical or cognitive conditions. These can impair an individual's ability to perform certain skills and engage in some activities. However, a person's disability does not necessarily prevent that person taking an active part in sport. Rather what happens in our social world is that people with disabilities are **negatively stereotyped** simply because they are disabled and as a result they are often treated differently.

Toolkit: Beliefs about sportspeople with disabilities

These activities are designed to investigate non-disabled people's beliefs about sportspeople with disabilities and physical activity.

1. Each member of your class should choose to represent a different group of disabled athletes, e.g. wheelchair users, amputees, a sensory disability or learning difficulties and then ask ten non-disabled people who are involved in your chosen sports to fill in the simple questionnaire below.

   Place either a Y for yes or N for No against each activity that you believe the above group is capable/incapable of participating in.

Sport/activity	Disabled group:	
	Y/N	If 'N' reason given
Football/Hockey		
Tennis		
Abseiling		
Sailing		
Basketball/Netball		
Skiing		
Marathon running		
Martial arts		
Horse riding		
Swimming		

Toolkit: Beliefs about sportspeople with disabilities (continued)

2. As a group draw up your results and findings and analyse whether any stereotypical view emerges.

    Use the diagram below:

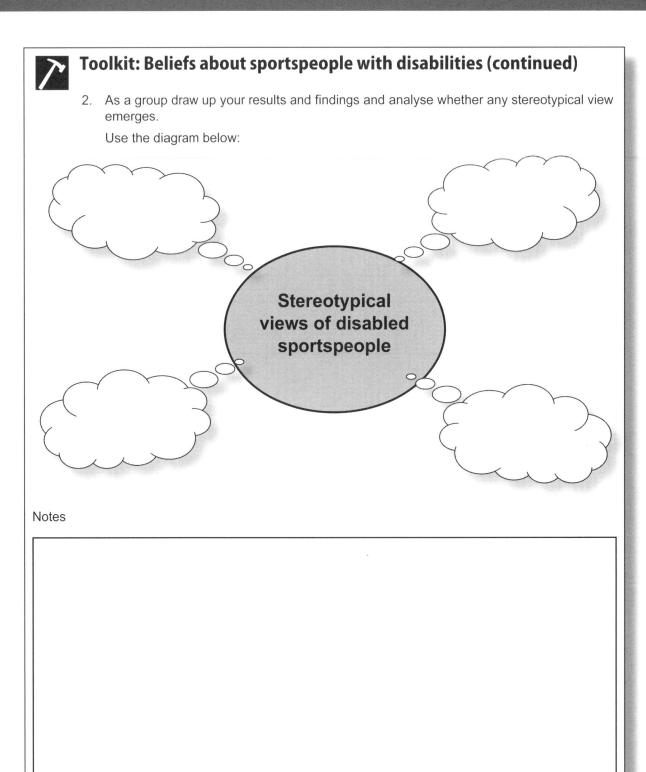

Notes

Toolkit: Beliefs about sportspeople with disabilities (continued)

3. Within your own choice of sports what attitudes emerged towards people with disabilities being involved in those sports.

a. _____

b. _____

c. _____

d. _____

Observe one session provided within your own choice of sports that either includes disabled athletes in it or is specifically put on for a disabled group. Research:

- the main barriers to the athlete's participation
- accessibility to the facility
- what adaptations has the facility made to accommodate the athletes
- what types of activities are carried out
- the range of specialist equipment
- how activities have been adapted to meet the needs of the participants
- the experience of the leader of the session
- how expensive it is
- what the athletes would like.

Author's advice

When you try to arrange a visit to any group you must be very sensitive and seek the permission and approval of the group for the visit. Do not assume they will want you to come.

You may know someone involved with disabled athletes in these sports. Your local authority may have a sports development officer for disabled sportspersons who could help you. You may need to contact either by phone or letter your local sports centre or activity organiser to see whether it would be possible to do this.

Useful websites are **www.disabilitysport.org.uk**, where you will be able to identify the regional development manger for your own area and **www.efds.net**, the national governing body for disability sport. Again, take some time to explore these sites. When you make contact, ask whether it would be possible for you to speak with the coaches and athletes about what they are doing.

The barriers that stop me and others being able to participate

From your research it is obvious that certain barriers have to be overcome to achieve equality of opportunity for all groups within society. Some of these may be attitudinal, emerging from the stereotypical myths about different groups, some may be economic barriers, and others may link to lack of facilities or access to those facilities.

 Toolkit: Barriers to participation

Individually or within your class identify different groups in your town or county that you think do not have the same access and opportunities to participate in sport and suggest why this is so.

Group	Reasons why participation is limited

Barriers to participation

A barrier is a factor that prevents individuals or groups from participating.

You have identified a variety of social influences that affect participation and non-participation in sport. You now need to identify the barriers to participation by people seeking access to specific sporting activities and provide examples from a number of different facilities or individuals.

 Toolkit: Identify barriers to your own participation in sport

Use the following headings below as a guideline. If you can think of additional barriers add them in.

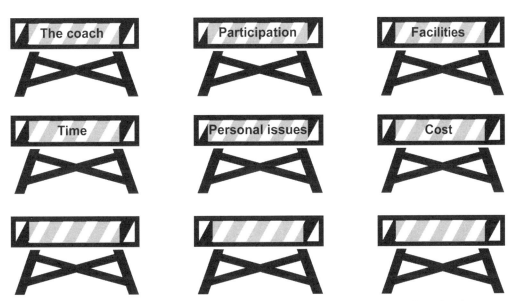

In small groups share your barriers to participation and regroup them all under the same headings.

These are of course very general barriers, but particular sports and particular groups will experience very specific barriers to inclusion.

Toolkit: Survey your chosen group

You are to undertake a survey of one of your identified groups, e.g. people with disabilities, unemployed or single parents, and investigate the reasons that are preventing them from becoming involved in one of your chosen sports.

You will need to survey as many of the group as you have the time to do. From this sample you will be able to draw some conclusions for your presentation.

Author's advice

You need to decide the best way to collect the information you require. Because it is a survey and you need to access a fair-sized sample it might be best to design another questionnaire.

Accessing particular groups might be difficult, but often your local authority leisure department will be able to put you in contact with particular community voluntary organisations involved in supporting such groups. Also visit your local leisure centres and find out what provision is being made there for particular groups.

As part of your IVA you have to provide some guidance on how sports organisations should address issues of barriers and non-participation and to identify the benefits this would have to the sport and to society in general.

One of the best ways that you can provide guidance is to present case studies or scenarios of initiatives that have been or could be undertaken to improve participation and examine how successful such initiatives have been and for what reasons. From these it is possible to draw up a list of "do's and don'ts" for initiatives.

On the following page is an example of what is meant by a case study:

Case study

The Do-Right Local Authority is keen to develop and promote girls' football. At present they do not have anyone with the expertise to do this. The chief executive of the authority, Mr Knowitall is a keen football fan and he knows a male coach, Ronnie Shouter, who has been coaching for 25 years and who is heavily involved in working with his son's football club. However, he has never been involved with girls' football. One Sunday after his son had scored the winning goal for the team, the chief executive thought it might be an idea to get this coach involved in the proposed girls' football project. Ronnie, after some discussion, agreed to help the local authority out.

He was eager to start and thought it might be a good starting point to organise a five-a-side competition for under-16 girls. Unfortunately, Sunday was the only evening that Ronnie was not involved in coaching his boys' groups and so the competition had to be at this time.

He decided to promote this event through the local schools and designed a poster that included the following:

How successful do you think the chief executive will be in getting his project off the ground and attracting young women and girls to participate?

Toolkit: Case studies for your sports

Using the above case study as a model you are to draw up two small case studies of initiatives to increase participation within your chosen sports that you can use as examples of good or poor practice.

You will need to research local initiatives within your chosen sports. To find out about these, you will need to contact your local sports councils, sports alliances, local authority, local sports centres and the governing bodies of your sports. These might provide you with the information needed to create a short case study or scenario.

Scenario 1

Scenario 2

Toolkit: Case studies for your sports (continued)

Within your class discuss the various scenarios and draw up reasons for the success or non-success of the particular case studies you have developed.

Initiative	Successful? Y/N	Reasons why

Author's advice

You should find this discussion very useful in drawing up guidelines on how to address barriers and non-participation.

This section has been concerned with examining important social influences that affect sport and how these impact upon the ability of individuals or groups to participate in sports of their choice. You should now be in a position to offer advice and guidance on how to increase participation.

Assessment activity (IVA) 2

As a Community Sports Development Officer you have been asked by local clubs for advice and guidance on how to increase participation in sport. You are to prepare a presentation that will involve bringing together the activities and additional research you have undertaken. Draw up some conclusions and recommendations in the following areas:

1. The different social influences – identify those that might affect whether individuals or groups of people take part in sport

2. Barriers to participation – recognition of those factors that prevent people from being able to take part in sport.

3. Finally, in your role as a Community Sports Development Officer, offer guidance by suggesting ways of overcoming these barriers.

Section 4: Where do I go for help?

LO4   The role of local, national and European agencies in promoting sport

In Britain, individual sports have developed independently and this has meant that we do not have a well-developed national sports policy. The development of the **Sports Council** in the early 1970s was the first attempt to develop such a national sports structure and policy. We have now moved a considerable way towards developing such structure. This involves a range of different local regional, national and international organisations and government agencies. **Sport England** has been given the remit to take the strategic lead for sport in England. It will be responsible for investing both lottery funding and money direct from the Government into sport.

In Europe, some of our sports have a European governing body that oversees competition at this level, e.g. football, athletics, swimming. With the growth of the European Union, sport will be increasingly influenced by European laws and practices. The most famous example of its influence has been in football where the **Bosman Ruling** changed the way professional sport is run.

You will need to collect and to put together information for local clubs that summarises the different types of sports initiatives that operate **or** are funded locally, nationally and at the European level. The next activity should enable you to gain an understanding of how that structure has developed and to identify some of the major agencies involved in the provision of sporting opportunities in Britain. You have already undertaken an investigation into the role and structure of the governing bodies of your chosen sports.

An agency is just an organisation established to promote the development of sport.

Toolkit: The organisation and structure of sport in the UK

Research information on the how sport in Britain is organised and structured. Then complete the organisational chart on the opposite page by placing the following agencies/organisation into their correct boxes:

Department of Culture Media and Sport

UK Sport

Sports England

CCPR

British Olympic Association

National Governing Bodies

Local Sports Clubs

International Olympic Committee

International Sports Federations, Schools and Universities

Recreation Departments

Sports Development Officers

Author's advice

You will find a number of useful sources of information to help you place the agencies in the right boxes. A good starting point again will be Sport England. It is responsible for investing both lottery funding and money direct from the Government into sport. Other useful sources are the websites for each of the agencies and you should familiarise yourself with these as it will help you to identify initiatives that have been developed. Make sure that you update your database to include these agencies.

Toolkit: The organisation and structure of UK sport (continued)

Complete the organisational chart by placing the agencies and organisations listed on the opposite page into their correct boxes.

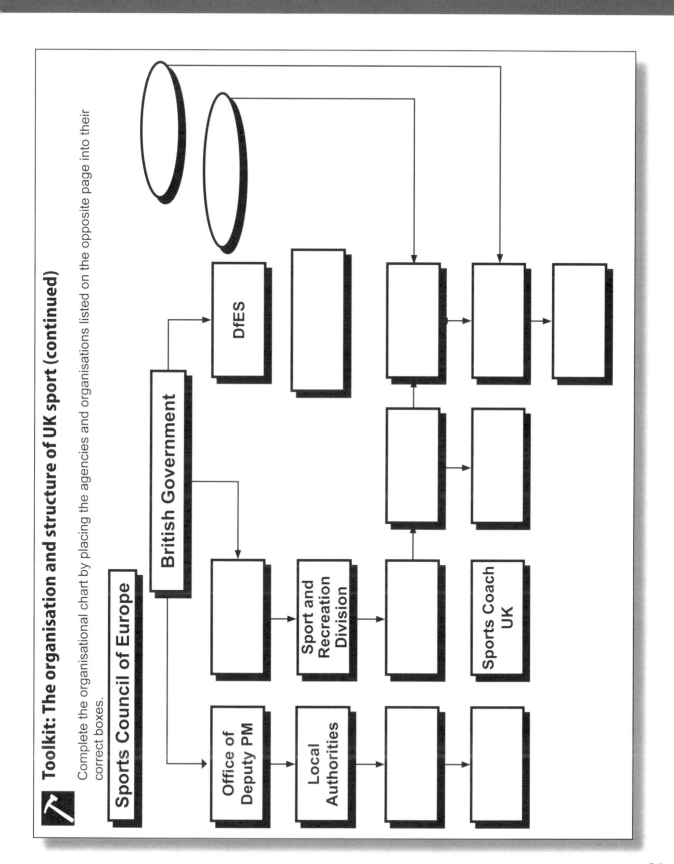

You now need to carry out some further research into various initiatives that are in place in preparation for either an interview or talk with a Sports Development Officer.

 Toolkit: Investigating initiatives and agencies

Research the following initiatives:

Initiative	Agency/agencies involved	Aims of the initiative	International/ national/regional/ local
Positive Futures			
Active Sports			
Sportsmark			
Sports leadership Awards			
TOPs programmes			
Step into Sport			
World Class Start			
Inclusive Fitness Initiative			
Europack			
Let's Kick Racism out of Football			
The Right to Play			
Football Solidarity Programme			

Tutor talk

Arrange for your local Community Sports Development Officer to come in and talk to the class about his or her role. Prepare as a group a number of questions that will help you identify both local and national initiatives that are at present being undertaken.

Try to cover some the following topics:

*   The Government strategy papers *A Sporting Future for All* and *Government Plan for Sport.*
*   Links between Central Government Policy and Community Sports Development Officers.
*   How Best Value and other government initiatives affect what they do.
*   How they assess the sporting needs of the local community.
*   What specifically these needs are.
*   What specific groups they target.
*   Initiatives they are at present involved with.
*   Other agencies that are involved in partnership with them.
*   Sports services they provide for the local community.
*   Links they have with other sectors of provision.
*   Major constraints on what they can provide.

Author's advice

It might be best to tape-record this interview so you can refer to it later.

This person will be a valuable source of information for you about what is happening in your local community and initiatives that are being undertaken.

You now have to develop your understanding of three particular initiatives: one local, one national and one European that aims to promote and develop sport. You have already gone some way towards developing an understanding of a local initiative both through the earlier research that you have done for overcoming barriers and also through you discussion with a local sports development officer.

Assessment activity (IVA) 3

Local initiatives

Visit an event or programme that is being run locally to promote and develop your own choice of sports. Find out as much information as you can about the event by carrying out interviews with participants and organisers to find out:

- what the event involved
- who was the target group was
- how many attended
- how they found out about it
- if they feel it has been a success
- if it could be improved.

National initiative

Research information about: an Active Schools, an Active Sport or an Active Communities project that is being run in your own region. You might like to combine this with the previous activity on a local initiative. Again, try to arrange a visit to the project and be prepared to ask questions to the organisers and the participants.

Produce a short report on your findings to cover the following:

- the aim of the initiative
- how successful it has been
- the impact on the community and/or individuals within the community
- how to improve or develop the initiatives.

 Author's advice

First you will need to get permission from the organisers to visit. Then to prepare an interview schedule for both participants and organisers. Interviewing is a skill that you have already had some practice at developing. What you are trying to find out here is how participants and organisers feel about the success of the event. You may want to tape-record your interview, but you must ask permission from those you interview before you start.

Europe

The Council of Europe (**www.coe.int**) is active on two fronts within sport:

1. to maintain the integrity of sport

2. to promote the virtues of sport.

It identifies three main areas of involvement:

- to promote sport for all

- to educate and fight against doping

- to foster tolerance through sport.

The Council's involvement is because member nations regard sport as important for the contribution it makes to the health of the population and the cohesive role it plays in society.

The European Union has a **Sports Unit** within the European Commission (**www.europa.eu.int**).

There are also international governing bodies of sport such as **Union of European Football Associations (UEFA)** (**www.uefa.com**) or the **International Olympic Committee (IOC)** (**www.olympic.org**) that may be involved in sport specific initiatives.

 Toolkit: Investigating a European-based sports initiative

Research on the Internet or specialist sports magazines and newspapers a European-based sports initiative. Describe what the initiative is about and assess whether it has been successful in achieving its objective.

Assessment activity (IVA) 4

Create an information booklet for local clubs that provides the following:

- The name and addresses of a range of agencies involved in the development and funding of sports initiatives.

- The name and aim of a range of local, regional and national and international initiatives at present being undertaken.

- Three short case studies of initiatives you have researched with an evaluation of how successful each has been.

The booklet should be produced in A5 format with an attractive, sports-related front cover.

Completing the Integrated Vocational Assignment

The culmination of your work in both **Sport in Society** and in **Ethics and Values** is the completion of your IVA, which is a compulsory part of your qualification. If you do not complete this you may not receive your certificate. Your tutor(s) or lecturer(s) will tell you how long you have to complete the IVA and the access you may have to resources.

Read the IVA carefully and make sure that you understand the work you should hand in and what is required of you. If you are uncertain, discuss it with your tutor(s).

The IVA requires you to work by yourself and to produce original work. You must not share your work with any other learners. If you work in a group at any time, you must present your own responses to each task for assessment.

Evidence can be a mix of written, videoed or taped material. Information taken from sources for research, e.g. the Internet and textbooks, must be identified and not presented as your own work. You should list the sources used. Some of the tasks you are required to complete may require either observation records or witness statements. You need to check with your tutor you have these and you must attach them to your submitted work.

Although the content of what you present is most important, you also need to consider the way you present it. You need to make the assessor's task as easy as possible. Remember he/she is marking many assignments, not just yours.

IVA completion checklist

	✓
Have you completed all the tasks?	
Are all tasks/sub-tasks labelled appropriately?	
Are all pages numbered and is your name on each one?	
Are tasks presented in correct order?	
Is all electronic material to be submitted in paper format?	
Have you clearly labelled video or audio tapes that you will submit as part of the assignment?	
Are all of your papers securely bound in a good quality wallet?	

Contents

Unit 2: The Reflective Practitioner

Introduction to the unit

Unit 2: Reflective Practitioner is a compulsory unit of the National Certificate/Diploma in Sport .

Reflective Practitioner gives you the opportunity to focus on yourself and what you can do to develop and progress in your chosen sport.

The unit is assessed internally, meaning that you will need to complete assignment work and generate evidence to cover the grading criteria.

Aims of the unit

Reflective Practitioner aims to enable a sports performer to consider their current performance. From this audit, you will be able to consider those aspects of your performance that are strengths and those that could be considered as weaknesses.

For both strengths and weaknesses, you will set yourself goals and targets for maintenance and improvements. You will need to monitor the progress you make against your intended goals over an agreed period of time. Throughout these monitoring reviews, you may need to revise targets accordingly based on your performance.

At the end of the unit, you will have developed the ability to reflect on your performances and plan for improvements. This is called **experiential learning**, i.e. learning through your own experience.

What the content will cover

In order to establish the facts about your current performance, you will need to get feedback from a variety of sources. These sources could include:

- your coach
- a team-mate, friend or peer
- parents
- own thoughts about your performance.

You will need feedback from at least two sources to help you establish a picture of where your strengths and weaknesses exist.

You will also need to consider the abilities and skills required by performers in your sport or, if a team game, specific skills for your usual position.

Once this has been carried out, you have a basis against which to consider what developments you need to make and where you can realistically progress to in the timescales covered by the unit.

You will then need to consider goal-setting. Goal-setting is the process by which you can determine how you are going to improve, the levels of improvement and how this can be measured over the timescales to ensure that progress is being made. This goal-setting process will include specific examples of drills and practices you will use to support your development, as well as identifying the people and facilities you can draw upon for support. The final aspect of goal-setting is your ability to identify the barriers that may inhibit your progress, how you can plan against these and ensure that you meet your intended targets or, where necessary, revised targets.

What will I do in class?

Classes will provide you with the underpinning knowledge required to complete each of the main assessment activities. This will take the form of formal lectures, class discussions, group work and a variety of exercises to develop your understanding of the purpose and benefits of reflecting on performances.

How will I be assessed?

In total, you will need to complete three main assessment activities. Each of these will concentrate on the following areas:

LO1:   **Assessment of current performance**

LO2:   **Targets for future performance**

LO3:   **Performance plan and barriers**

LO4:   **Monitor and evaluation of performance**

For each assessment activity you will have an individual deadline to meet. All work will need to be word processed wherever possible. By the nature of the unit, the evidence can be self-written, photographs, witness statements, match reports, etc. You will need to be able to use various software applications to support the production of evidence for assessment including Microsoft Excel.

What must I submit?

In total, you will submit evidence of assessing your current performance in your sport, an action plan of how to develop areas you identify and finally, a review of how effective this action plan has been.

 Author's advice

Reflective Practitioner is a unit that requires self-discipline and motivation. Unlike other units, you will not need to spend hours carrying out research for assignments. However, this does not mean that the unit is a soft option. You will have deadlines that need to be met and the most important element of the unit is honesty – by being honest with yourself you stand to gain the most from completing the unit.

It is suggested that you work little and often on this unit to allow you to focus on your performances, developments, targets and barriers over an agreed time period. By monitoring your performances over time, you will build up a far clearer picture of your strengths and weaknesses as well as recognising what training, activities and drills are of most benefit to you based on your actual needs.

What is a reflective practitioner?

The process of reflection is based upon using our experiences in sport to assess what areas are in need of improvement and what we can do to facilitate this improvement. Reflection is an active and on-going process by which you will seek and use feedback from others and analyse your own performances.

Whilst the activities you will be involved in during this unit may be the first time you've formally reflected on your performance, it will support you in considering which specific aspects of your performance can be improved and in finding you the most effective methods to make this improvement happen.

Reflection is considered to be a cycle of experiences that support our learning and make it more effective. **David Kolb** proposed the following model in 1984.

Kolb's Learning Cycle explains how an experience can lead to improved performance. This cycle can be applied to all aspects of life not just sport.

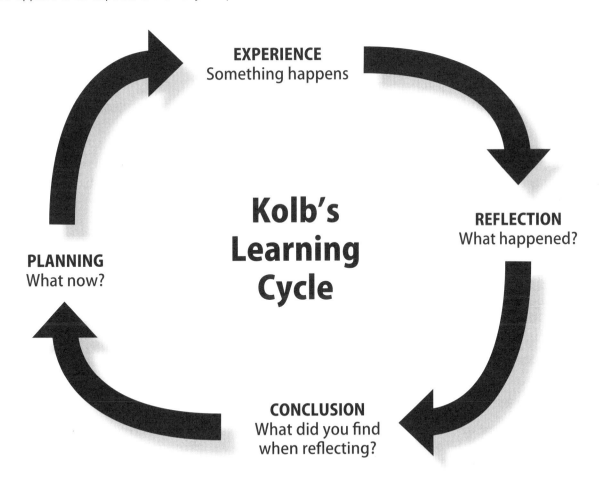

The diagram of Kolb's Learning Cycle should help you understand how the reflection process works. This means that we are constantly reflecting in one form or another. You may have found yourself thinking about your performance, but not written anything down. The use of Kolb's Learning Cycle can help you understand how to make your reflection more purposeful and shape your training to specific areas in need of development.

Reflective planning for progression

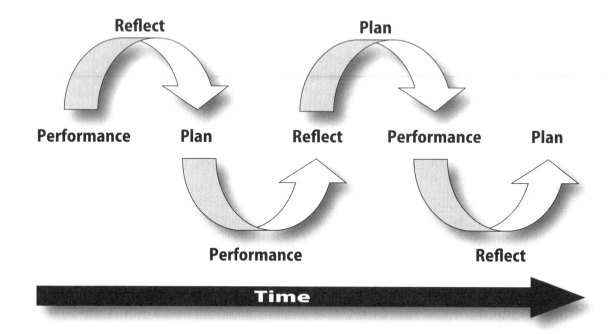

Kolb's cycle demonstrates the process of reflecting on our performances. However, it doesn't allow for you to show where you have made progress and possibly improved your performances as a result of reflecting and planning your training to focus on specific areas.

In the beginning

It is essential that you establish some of the factors that have affected you in your participation in sport. This includes detailing why you initially got involved, what and who encouraged you to take part in your sport and what benefits you have taken from your involvement.

By completing this exercise you have started to examine your motivation for sports involvement. You will also have identified the people that have been part of this process and how their actions influenced you.

Getting started

There are wide varieties of reasons for people getting involved in sports. These could include social factors such as the influence of friends, teachers and or parents; the influence of a role model can also have an impact on what sport a young performer chooses to be involved in. Internal factors for taking up a sport can include the desire for recognition, a performer's interest and their attitude towards competitive situations.

National governing bodies of sport are keen to engage performers in their sport and to ensure that they are able to enjoy their experiences and keep taking part. To help support this process, coaching qualifications are being evolved, which include fun games and activities that help young performers learn skills in an enjoyable way. Clubs are encouraging their coaching staff to achieve these qualifications

As an incentive to clubs that develop in line with National Governing Bodies and general sports bodies' guidelines, **Charter** marks can be awarded in recognition of a club's efforts.

To start the process of considering the background factors to you being involved in sport, it would be worthwhile reflecting on your early sports experiences.

Toolkit: Early experiences in sport

With a friend, talk about your early experiences in sport. Consider the factors that made you want to be involved. Produce a list of the reasons. Then consider the people that influenced you, listing how their influence impacted upon you.

Use the tables below to take your notes.

Factors that encouraged you to be involved in sport.

Make new friends			

Who influenced you and how?

Who?	How?
School Teacher	After school coaching and lunch time activities

When you have collated your lists, share your findings with the group. List down any factors shared during the discussion that don't appear on your own list.

At this point, it is worth considering the nature of the factors that have motivated you to be involved in sport. These can be placed into two categories.

- **intrinsic** motivation

- **extrinsic** motivation.

Motivation is linked to the rewards we receive. For example, if you are motivated by beating a previous time rather than the winning of a medal or trophy then you are being influenced by **intrinsic** factors.

Intrinsic motivation

A 45-year old woman starts to run to get fit. After a few months, she sets herself a target of running in the local 10km charity run in three months' time. She trains and sets herself a target time for the charity run. In the 10km run she beats her target time. Although she didn't win the race, she feels great satisfaction in her accomplishment and is motivated to continue in her sport.

Extrinsic motivation

Sport provides many opportunities to receive rewards in the form of medals, trophies, certificates and cups. Extrinsic rewards also include acknowledgement by others. For example a young performer that receives praise and encouragement from a coach and uses this to motivate themselves further is being influenced by extrinsic factors.

Referring back to your list, which factors do you consider have the greater influence on your involvement in sport, intrinsic or extrinsic?

Role models

A role model can be a powerful motivator to a performer of any age. Seeing someone in your sport can support you in your development. For example, watching someone overcome a barrier such as injury or winning against high level opponents can help your own efforts. This type of experience is called a **vicarious experience**.

Toolkit: Investigating role models

Investigate a particular role model from your sport. Read articles from newspapers about them and their performances, watch videos of them in action and if available read any books written about them. Having this type of insight into a role model can help you understand what challenges they have had to meet and how they overcame specific barriers to their development.

List role models and identify what makes them a role model to you.

Sporting role model	Characteristics you most admire

Section 1: Knowing me···knowing you

LO1:   Assess current performance in a chosen sport

What's the story?

Reflective practice has become a focal point for performance assessment in a diverse range of situations. The underlying principle behind it is that we learn through experience and by reflecting on these experiences we can improve. Reflective practice is used in business, education and has become important in sport. Sports science has seen an explosion in the ways in which performers are assessed and monitored and training methods are starting to reflect the principles science has applied. A progression from the physical science was that of social or psychological science, where the performers state of mind was as crucial to outcomes as their physical state. Reflective practice is very much about establishing a balanced picture of our performances and responding to factual observations.

In it to win it

By being a reflective practitioner you will establish an understanding of your own performance. You will be able to do this by asking others about your performance, thinking about yourself and considering the components that make up your sports performance.

From this balanced picture you will be able to identify specific areas that are in need of development to help improve your all-round performances. This will mean specific drills with predetermined targets. Once you have these targets agreed and set out, you will be able to recognise progress and feel more confident about yourself. Confidence is recognised as a cornerstone of performance.

By the end of the unit delivery, you will be able to work independently and start to be more involved in your own development. You will also start to be more sure about yourself and develop a sense of self-efficacy, one step further than self-confident.

Performance CV

The first exercise to be carried out is a look back at your sporting achievements that have enabled you to participate in your sport. This "audit" will detail in chronological order (most recent last) your experiences. For example, if you have represented a school, county or club at any level, this experience is a contributory factor to you being involved in your sport. It has influenced the way in which you have progressed to the point at which you find yourself today.

This piece of work will be entitled "Background to Development" and will be presented as a series of bullet points with a brief explanation of the experience gained.

For example:

* August 2002–June 2004: County Schools Squad. Competing in regional and national competitions on a regular basis and working with some of the best coaches in the county. This experience enabled me to develop a technical understanding of my sport and helped me gain confidence when competing against capable opponents.

You can use the above statement as a template and customise it to fit your own circumstances and experiences.

Author's advice

Remember that good presentation can help you and your readers' understanding of the points you are trying to make. Take the time to use IT skills; ideally, this should be produced using Microsoft Word or a similar word processing package. Do not add graphics or clip art at this point. However, if you wish to add a picture of yourself that is relevant to the experiences being detailed, then that will be a positive thing to include. Also, if you have newspaper cuttings that relate to a specific event, then these too can be included. If necessary, you can scan these and resize them to fit your purpose. If you are using a word processing software application, you must ensure that you run a spell check and, equally important, proof read your work to avoid any "typos". Once you have completed the work, submit it to your tutor.

Tutor talk

If you need to develop IT skills to help you out in the process mentioned above, speak to your tutors about how you can do this. You should have access to a Learning Resource Centre at your college at which you can ask for advice and help in putting together documents using a variety of programmes such as Microsoft Word and Excel. You can even take extra qualifications in IT that will be useful in your time as a student and when you start full-time employment.

Me as a performer

The **audit** completed for the last exercise will have enabled you to reflect on the experiences that have brought you to today and your involvement in your sport. In this part of your work, you will need to focus on yourself and the components that combined to make you into what and who you are. One of the first steps in this is considering the skills and abilities required to play your sport and, if appropriate, those specific to your position.

Specific sports demand a specific set of skills and abilities to be able to compete at any level. In addition to this, in team games certain positions, roles, etc, demand a unique set of skills. For example, a tennis player will require different skills to a badminton player (although there are some similarities in the demands of the sports). Another example is that of a fullback in rugby. The fullback will have a different role from a prop and as such will need to train on different aspects of the same sport.

In the next Toolkit, you will need to consider the skills and abilities of successful sports people in your chosen sport. For example, if you play as a goalkeeper in football, you will be able to include skills such as communication, bravery, anticipation, catching and jumping skills.

Toolkit: Skills, abilities and traits to compete

List as many of the skills and abilities required to compete in your sport and (if applicable) in your preferred position. The suggested way to present this is in the form of a spider diagram.

This exercise represents a list of words that are specific to you and your sport/position. The example below will give you some pointers to how you may want your own project to look.

The points above are far from exhaustive and you may want to have several different sheets reflecting on the different roles you fulfil in your sport. The list you produce will be the start of the first main assessed point when you will need to focus on your own current levels of performance.

 ## Author's advice

Use IT skills to present this. If you are using **Microsoft Word** you will need to have the **Drawing toolbar** on the screen. To get this, go to the **View menu** on the **Main menu bar** and select **Toolbars**, **Drawing** is found here. Select **Drawing** and the toolbar will appear on the screen. You can draw shapes; insert **Word Art** quickly from this toolbar. If you want to add text to a shape you have drawn, simply click the **right-mouse button** on the shape and select **Add text**.

Body types

This audit could include your body type. In 1940, **Sheldon** developed an accurate means to classify body type. He introduced three main classifications:

Endomorph	**Mesomorph**	**Ectomorph**

Endomorph	Mesomorph	Ectomorph
Round and soft body	Muscular body	Tall and thin
'Pear' shaped	Wedge shaped	High forehead
Rounded head	Wide and broad shoulders	Narrow shoulders, chest, abdomen and hips
Wider front to back rather than side to side	Low levels of body fat	Little muscle or fat
High levels of body fat		

Sheldon determined a performer's body type by scoring them on a scale of 1 to 7 for each classification. Each performer would be given a score.

For example: 4-3-3 (the order of this scoring is Endomorph – Mesomorph – Ectomorph).

Extremes are easily scored:

An extreme Endomorph is 7-1-1

An extreme Mesomorph is 1-7-1

and

An extreme Ectomorph is 1-1-7

Toolkit: What body type are you?

Ask your tutor to give you a score between 1 and 7 for each of the three areas Sheldon uses to create a description of a performer's body type. Once you have done this, ask a friend to score you too. You can then score yourself and compare the results.

Use the table below to record the scores given.

Source	Endomorph score	Mesomorph score	Ectomorph score
Tutor			
Friend			
Me			

Research has suggested that the certain body types and scores are associated with specific sports. For example:

A high jumper would score in the range of 2 – 6 – 2 to 2 – 3 – 6.

Body Mass Index

The **Body Mass Index** (**BMI**) categorises your height and weight. It doesn't take into account muscle development, e.g. a muscular athlete may be classified as overweight when completing this index. You can calculate whether you're height and weight are appropriate by examining your BMI score. To calculate your BMI score complete the following equation:

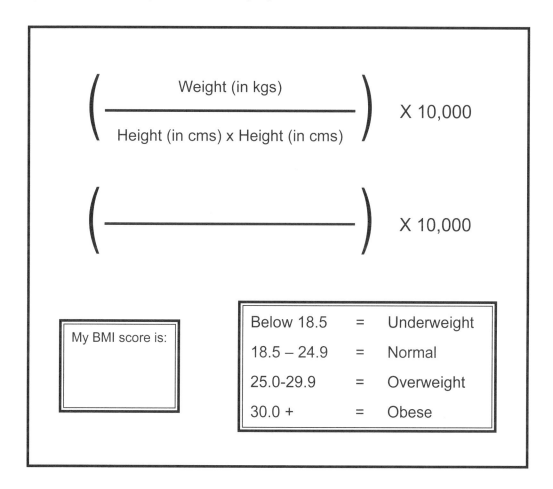

$$\left(\frac{\text{Weight (in kgs)}}{\text{Height (in cms) x Height (in cms)}} \right) \times 10,000$$

$$\left(\underline{\hspace{6cm}} \right) \times 10,000$$

My BMI score is:

Below 18.5	=	Underweight
18.5 – 24.9	=	Normal
25.0-29.9	=	Overweight
30.0 +	=	Obese

Note: There are a number of different BMI scales that you can use. The one included here is indicative only. Other scores can be obtained from numerous online BMI calculators.

Lifestyle

Lifestyle can have a significant impact on performance. Alcohol, smoking, drugs, sleep patterns, etc, will all have an effect on the results you are able to achieve.

A balanced diet, plenty of physical rest, avoiding excessive alcohol, smoking and recreational drugs will help you achieve the best results. This is often an aspect of performance that is ignored by many non-elite performers. A good diet can be achieved by adhering to the food pyramid (see diagram).

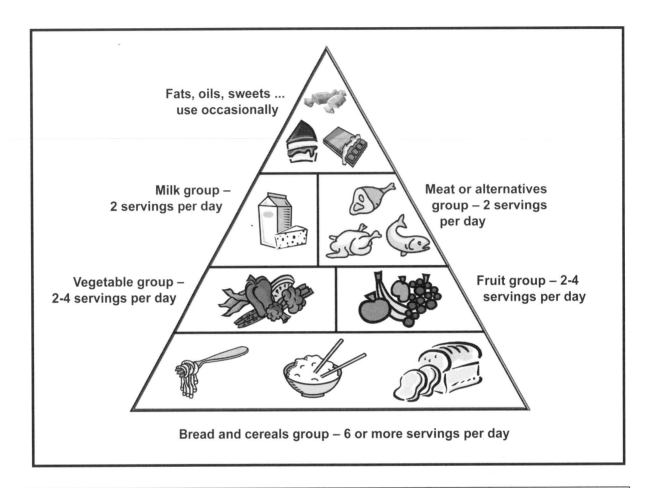

Fats, oils, sweets ...
use occasionally

Milk group –
2 servings per day

Meat or alternatives
group – 2 servings
per day

Vegetable group –
2-4 servings per day

Fruit group – 2-4
servings per day

Bread and cereals group – 6 or more servings per day

 Toolkit: Monitoring your eating habits

Monitor your eating habits over a week. What do you eat and when? What time are you eating breakfast? Are you eating a balanced diet or are you eating too much salt, too many fats and not enough fibre? You may be surprised by your findings.

If you consider your diet to be a factor that needs improving, it may be worth keeping a diary of what you eat and when, and reflect on this. If you notice that there is much room for improvement, make diet one of the areas for your action plan.

It is also worth noting some of the recommended daily intakes of calories, fat and salt. A new skill to develop would be understanding the information on food packaging about levels of fats, colourings, etc, that products contain.

There is plenty of up to date information available on healthy diets. Much of this is a result of the Government's desire to see reductions in the levels of obesity in the UK population.

For more information on what constitutes a balanced and healthy diet, visit the **British Nutrition Foundation** website (**www.nutrition.org.uk**).

Other websites worth a look include the **Food Standards Agency** official website (**www.food.gov.uk**), which is full of interesting facts and useful information about good eating habits, and **www.salt.gov.uk**, also from the Food Standards Agency, which explains how too much salt can triple the chances of a person suffering from coronary heart disease and how 85% of men and 69% of women eat too much salt each day.

Personality and imagery

Allport (1937) defined personality as:

> *"The dynamic organisation within the individual of those psychophysical systems that determine his unique adjustments to the environment."*

A more simple definition is offered by *Hollander (1971)*:

> *"The sum total of an individual's characteristic which make him unique."*

The uniqueness of our personalities means that we will respond to certain situations in a unique manner. For example, concentration is an area that is key to all sports performers. A cricketer may not be involved in any action for a prolonged period of time, but then be expected to perform effectively at a moment's notice.

Another unique element of our personality is our ability to cope with anxiety, stress and pressure when performing. A good example of this was seen during Euro 2004 when Zinedine Zidane was physically sick shortly before taking a crucial last minute penalty against England. Despite the enormous pressure, Zidane scored and won the match. Jonny Wilkinson found himself in a similar moment in the last minutes of the Rugby World Cup final in 2003.

Anxiety can act as a barrier to good performance. One way of helping a performer overcome anxiety is mental practice. Mental practice or visualisation allows a performer to imagine themselves in a given situation and be able to feel relaxed. Just as Wilkinson would have practised kicking a ball to get his technique correct, he would have practised mentally to help his actions become automatic and to block out unnecessary distractions such as noise from the crowd.

 Tutor talk

There are a number of simple tests that can assess your personality. Tests by **Eysenck** and **Cattell** can be completed in lectures. Ask your tutor to arrange for these tests to be used in a lecture and record your results.

You can also look at specific tests to measure your anxiety in competitive situations. Your tutor can direct you towards which tests are the simplest to administer and score.

Imagery

Imagery is a well-used tool in helping develop sports performers and reduce anxiety. Imagery can be used in training and pre- and post-competition. You can even mentally practice immediately before competition to help you feel relaxed and confident.

Toolkit: How do you use imagery?

Step 1:　Lie down, get comfortable, close your eyes and relax. Start breathing slowly and focus on your breathing, block out any noises or distractions. You can listen to music to help you to relax. If you do listen to music try and choose a relaxing track without lyrics and keep the volume low. Wiggle your fingers and toes to help relax. If you still feel tense, tighten your muscles again and slowly relax your body. Repeat this process for as long as necessary to get yourself relaxed.

Step 2:　Imagine yourself in a situation that makes you feel relaxed, e.g. on a beach. Create a clear image where you can see colours and details of what is happening in your imagined scene.

Step 3:　Listen to sounds, notice any smells. If you are imagining yourself on a beach, try to feel the warmth of the sun on your skin or pushing the sand between your toes.

Step 4:　Focus on an aspect of your sports performance. Imagine watching yourself in your sport. Follow steps 2 and 3 linking to your sport. For example, feeling yourself catching a ball or holding a racket.

Step 5:　Slowly start to concentrate on your breathing again. Count each breath, after ten counts, open your eyes and get used to the light in the room.

Once you have "come round", walk around the room to get used to where you are. As soon as possible, write down the observations of your visualisation session. If you think that anxiety has a detrimental impact on your performance, visualisation could be very beneficial to you.

Imagine yourself on a beach, try to feel the warmth of the sun on your skin or pushing the sand between your toes

Fitness and recovery

Fitness is crucial to successful and effective performance. Being fit can help a performer avoid injury, concentrate for longer periods and be able to recover from efforts in training and matches. This is especially important in sports where effort is not consistent, e.g. rugby, hockey, football, etc.

You can measure the various components of your fitness easily via a number of methods. For example, you can complete a multi-stage fitness test (also known as a bleep test), a 12-minute run, explosive strength test, flexibility tests or monitor your heart rate over a period of exercise.

Toolkit: Harvard step test

How to take the test.

Step up on to a standard gym bench once every two seconds for five minutes (150 steps).

1. Have someone to help you keep to the required pace.

2. One minute after finishing the test take your pulse rate (count for 30 seconds) – Pulse 1.

3. Two minutes after finishing the test take your pulse rate (count for 30 seconds) – Pulse 2.

4. Three minutes after finishing the test take your pulse rate (count for 30 seconds) – Pulse 3.

To calculate your results you must complete the following equation:

score = (100 x total number of seconds in the test) ÷ (2 x (total BPM in the recovery periods))

For example:

$$5 \text{ mins x } 60 \text{ secs} = 300 \text{ secs}$$

$$(100 \text{ x } 300) \div (2 \text{ x total BPMs})$$

Record your results and then put them into the table below.

Pulse 1 after 1 minute 30 seconds	
Pulse 2 after 2m 30s	
Pulse 3 after 3m 30s	
Total BPMs	

Final score:

How to rate your score:

80 plus = Good

65-79 = Above average

56 - 64 = Below average

Less than 55 = Poor

Flexibility

 Toolkit: Sit and reach test

If you wish to use this test as a means of estimating your flexibility, you will need the following:

- A friend to take the measurements and offer encouragement.
- A **sit and reach box**.
- A ruler or similar to push along the surface of the sit and reach box if no measurements are indicated on box itself.

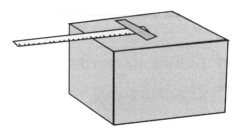

A sit and reach test involves sitting on the floor with legs out straight ahead. Place both your feet against a sit and reach box (remember to take your shoes off and to keep your knees flat to the floor. Then lean forward and, as slowly and smoothly as possible, push your fingers along the table as far as you can reach. To be a valid score, the stretch must be held for at least two seconds. Take the measurement from the point of your fingertips.

Watch out for:

- knees bending
- hands not being level on the measuring surface
- unsteady movements.

Note: Warm up thoroughly before taking this test.

How to score

You will need to measure the distance to or beyond your toes. A score that shows the distance before your toes is recorded as a negative; any measurement past your toes is recorded as a positive. The table shows how your can classify your scores – all scores are in centimetres.

	Men (cms)	Women (cms)
Superb	> +27	> +30
Excellent	+17 to +27	+21 to +30
Good	+6 to +16	+11 to +20
Average	0 to +5	+1 to +10
Fair	-8 to -1	-7 to 0
Poor	-19 to -9	-14 to -8
Very poor	< -20	< -15

Multi-stage fitness test

Toolkit: Taking a bleep test

This test is known under a number of different names, the most commonly used is the **bleep test**. The bleep test is made up of a series of stages and involves running between two marked areas. You must be able to run from one end of the "court" to the other (at least 20 metres) and turn in time with the bleep.

To take the test:

1. You will need a recorded "bleep". This can be found on a multi-stage fitness test tape or CD. Your tutor may have access to one of these and you should ask for this to be part of a reflective practitioner class.

2. Find a friend to note down the number of runs you and the level of bleeps you achieve.

3. Start with your feet behind the start marker.

4. Run between the markers and make sure that you arrive at the next marker before the next bleep.

5. If you arrive at a marker before hearing the bleep, wait for it before you start the next run.

6. Carry on running for as long as possible, until you can no longer keep up with the speed set by the tape/CD.

8. As the test progresses, the time between the bleeps reduces and therefore the pace you need to run at increases. Carry on running until you can no longer keep up with the bleeps.

9. If you fail to reach the end of the shuttle before the bleep, try two or three more runs to make up the pace before the test is finished.

If your fitness is something that you want to improve and you feel that the bleep test is a good measure, you can complete one test and record your score. You can then train for a period of time and take the test again. If your training has been effective, you should see an increase in your scores.

At least 20 metres

Sergeant Jump

 Toolkit: Taking a Sergeant Jump test

A Sergeant Jump looks to give a measure of your explosive power. To complete a Sergeant Jump, you will need the following equipment:

- a wall to measure your jump against
- a piece of chalk
- a tape to measure the distance of your jump.

To start the test, you will need to stand against the wall with you feet flat to the floor. You must then reach up with your arm and mark the wall with a piece of chalk.

Take a step away from the wall and jump vertically, you can bend your legs as you need and use your arms to help power the jump. Try to mark the wall at the highest point of your jump. You can then measure the difference between the two chalk marks.

Scoring

In order to give you a good indication of your explosive power, take three measurements and calculate an average in the differences. Once you have this figure, use the scoring grid below.

Rating	Males (cm)	Females (cm)
Excellent	70 and above	60 and above
Very good	61-70	51-60
Above average	51-60	41-50
Average	41-50	31-40
Below average	31-40	21-30
Poor	21-30	11-20
Very poor	Below 21	Below 11

If you wish to improve on this score, you can complete the test on a regular basis along side a training programme that seeks to increase your explosive strength. Through this, you can measure your improvements.

Learning style

Learning style is the term used to describe the most effective way for you to develop knowledge and understanding of a skill or ability. Being able to recognise your dominant learning style will enable you to learn quickly and efficiently, saving time by avoiding a style that is not necessarily effective for you.

If you can develop skills and abilities quickly, it will mean that your performance will improve more quickly and you will develop a greater sense of achievement and self-confidence. You will also be able to avoid some frustrations in your development by using drills, practices and training routines that best match your learning style. Additionally, you will be able to work with your coach and possibly adapt the training to meet your needs. In team sports, this may be difficult to achieve, as the coach must try to meet the learning styles of the entire squad!

 Tutor talk

You may have completed a learning style analysis in the first couple of weeks of your course. If you did, make a note of the dominant style identified in that test. Your tutor may have recorded your results and may be able to provide you with a copy of your paper.

Your learning style will affect how you carry out your assignment work. Ask yourself some questions, such as the following:

- Do I like to work in a quiet room with few distractions?
- Do I like to work with music playing in the background?
- Do I prefer doing rather than thinking about things?

The answers to these questions could provide you with some pointers to your dominant learning style. Typically, tests will look to score you in three main styles:

- visual
- kinaesthetic
- auditory.

Each style has unique characteristics that you can use to help you understand the most effective way for you to work, train and practice.

Toolkit: Finding out your learning style

Using the table below read the scenario and decide which of the three statements best matches the way in which you prefer to learn. Place a tick against the most relevant statement.

Remembering something	I need to write something down if I'm going to remember it. ☐	If I study and talk out loud, I remember the information. ☐	I find it easier to remember something if I practice it repeatedly. ☐
When talking to people	I find it helps me if I look at someone when they are talking to me. ☐	I can still follow what is being said even if I appear to be looking away. ☐	I'll use my hands to emphasise points and I like to touch people when I talk to them. ☐
Writing something down	I try and see the word, especially if I'm trying to remember how to spell something. ☐	I may talk out loud or talk to myself as I write the information down. ☐	I do take notes, but very rarely go back to them and read through. ☐
Concentrating in class	I'm not easily distracted. ☐	I'm easily distracted, especially by noise. ☐	My mind wanders in class and I find myself daydreaming if I'm not involved in a class. ☐
Reading	I like reading descriptive words and will picture characters, places and situations. ☐	I like reading dialogue and will imagine listening to the characters talking. ☐	I like reading about action although, generally, I'm not a big reader. ☐
Assessment work	I like to go back over my notes and handouts highlighting relevant information. ☐	I like to work with someone and talk about the assignment tasks. ☐	I prefer to work away from a desk and have music playing in the background. ☐
Note taking	I take a lot of notes on what I hear and what I read. ☐	I prefer to talk about things than writing them down. I will read through my notes to help me understand. ☐	My notes are often messy and poorly organised, although I do know where information is. ☐
Getting to a new place	I prefer to use a map or drawn directions to find somewhere. ☐	I like to memorise a route in a step-by-step manner and have someone read directions out to me. ☐	Once I know where I need to go, I like to try and get there. ☐
Number of ticks	V	A	K

V = Visual As a visual learner you like to receive information presented visually in a written format. This includes diagrams, pictures, graphics, tables, maps and charts.

A = Auditory As an auditory learner you will prefer to receive language presented in the spoken word. This will include talking aloud to yourself.

K = Kinaesthetic As a kinaesthetic learner you will learn most effectively if a task involves you being engaged in an active and/or physical manner.

Has completing this test presented any surprises?

Sources of feedback

As part of the audit process you will need feedback and information about your current levels of performance from a variety of sources. This information can come from the following:

- Your own thoughts and perceptions about your performance.
- Observations by your coach.
- Observations made by team-mates.
- Observations made by friends, parents and peers.
- Interviews with any of the above.
- Video analysis.

Information taken from all of these sources will enable you to develop a sound understanding of what elements of your performances can be considered as strengths and which are in need of development and practice.

Observations can be made formal and you can record performances in a tally chart. For example, if you were playing as a central defender in football you may want to assess your performance in the following areas:

- Tackling
- Passing – long
- Heading
- Passing – short

By having someone watch you, you can find out more about your performance than you can through trying to record how you played after a match. You may also want to break down the match into several sections; this will allow you to consider when you are performing effectively and or the impact of fitness and fatigue on your performance.

An example of a tally chart for this example is as follows:

Timings/ component	1st half			2nd half			Total
	0–15 mins	16–30 mins	31–45 mins	46–60 mins	61–75 mins	76–90 mins	
Successful tackle	III	IIII	I	III	II	IIII	17
Unsuccessful tackle	I	II	IIII	III	IIII	IIII	18
Successful Header	III	II	II	IIII	IIII	II	17
Unsuccessful header	I	I	III	III	I	IIII	13
Successful short pass	III	IIII	IIII	III	IIII	II	20
Unsuccessful short pass	I	II	I	II	III	IIII	13
Successful long pass	IIII	II	I	I	II	I	11
Unsuccessful long pass	I	III	IIII	III	II	IIII	17

You can use this type of match analysis to target specific areas of your performance that are in need of improvement. The data would be useful if the analysis was carried out over a number of matches.

Using the table above, what conclusions would you form?

Which areas do you consider this performer is in need of working on and why?

Author's advice

By carrying out this type of observation, you can start to identify areas of your performances that may need to be improved upon in your action plan. It can provide as ideal evidence for your first assignment activity. You can create your own observation template, which is specific to you, and ask a coach or friend to complete the observations for you. These completed templates can then be submitted with your assignment work.

SWOT analysis

SWOT stands for:

Strengths

Weaknesses

Opportunities

Threats

The analysis is usually presented in the format of a box:

Strengths	Weaknesses
Opportunities	Threats

The notion of a SWOT analysis is to identify areas where performance can be improved. The strengths and weaknesses are internal and include fitness, diet, etc, while the opportunities and weaknesses are external and include factors such as access to facilities, college work, etc.

A SWOT analysis is a simple method to employ when assessing your own current levels of performance. As part of **assessment activity 1**, a SWOT analysis would be an ideal tool for self-assessment.

Assessment activity 1

Assessment activity one covers the following learning outcome:

LO1: Assess current performance in a chosen sport

In order to complete this task, you must use **TWO** methods of assessing your current levels of performance.

You can employ any two of the following methods:

- Peer assessment/ observation
- Self-assessment
- Coach assessment/ observation
- Interviews

- Audit of skills and abilities
- Match analysis
- SWOT analysis

You will need to submit records and documentation to support observations and summarise the information within the main body of the assignment text.

The aspects to consider when assessing your current levels of performance include:

- Prior experience
- Technical knowledge and skills
- Technical ability
- Levels of fitness

- Commitment
- Training attendance and effort
- Access to equipment and facilities
- Access to effective coaching

- Team working skills
- Leadership and communication skills
- Diet
- Values and beliefs

 Author's advice

You must avoid trying to complete any assessment work on the night before the hand-in date! Reflective Practitioner is not a unit that can be completed overnight, it does require you to relax and think about your performances.

Remember the importance of professional standards when submitting your work. Refer back to **Study tip** in the introduction for some hints and advice on what to submit.

Section 2: Beat my goal

LO2: Explore targets for future performance in a chosen sport

LO3: Produce an effective performance plan taking into account barriers to achievement

Goal-setting and targets – an introductory text

Goal-setting allows a performer to be clear about what they want to achieve. This clarity of focus enables considered and thoughtful planning that is specific to the desired outcomes of the performer.

Michael Johnson won Olympic gold in 1996 in the 200 and 400 metres. He considered that goal-setting was a significant factor in his success. In his book *Slaying the Dragon* Johnson recognises how goal-setting supported him in utilising his talent effectively. Johnson gives the budding goal-setter five tips in using goals effectively:

1. Dream small

Think like a sprinter, in small increments. If your eventual goal is the Olympics, set goals along the path – "Improve my 800m time by 1 second"; "Make the High school track team". Short-term goals are the only reliable path.

2. Write down your goals

This makes it formal and gives notice to yourself and others that the work has officially begun. And it keeps your goals clear and in focus

3. Be specific

If your goal is to "get in shape" you will – bad shape! It is far better to focus on specific goals, like "run a seven minute mile." Or "do 50 sit-ups a day". In the office, "Finish the Wilkinson Report by May 1" works; "get caught up at work" does not.

4. Be realistic

You can accomplish most things you set out to do, but it will take time. Don't shoot for something unattainable – completely outside of your nature or opportunity. At least not right away.

5. Know yourself

Find your core, that thing you are chasing. Set goals based on what you really want, not what other people expect of you. Don't assume that goals are only for the competitive areas of your life. You can make goals for family, relationships, anything.

Text from p.20 Slaying the Dragon by Michael Johnson, © 1996 by Michael Johnson Reprinted by permission of HarperCollins Publishers Inc.

Recent research has suggested that goal-setting by athletes has helped achieve higher levels of performance.

Why does goal-setting work?

It's always good to have a vision of what you want to achieve. This may relate to fitness, weight loss, winning an Olympic medal or achieving a set standard of performance; but you also need a plan for how you are going to attain this goal.

Goals can help to motivate you and give you a target to aim for. However, it is important that you are very specific about what you are trying to achieve and realistic about what can be achieved. Having an unrealistic goal can mean that you become demotivated. Whilst your planning process may not involve Olympic gold or national representative levels, they are important to you and your development. It is also important to avoid making goals too easy as this can reduce the amount of benefit you can take from the experience.

To help you in the planning process, you must take ownership of each goal you set. You can work in collaboration with your coach, but all goals must be based on what you want to get out of your performances. You can also monitor your progress far more effectively if you are fully aware of what you are trying to achieve. You can also recognise the progress made towards your final target throughout the time period covered by your action plan.

Monitoring your progress helps motivate you to continue to achieve. If progress is slower than expected, the monitoring process helps you adjust your training programme to increase your development and achievements. The specific nature of goals can also help you in confronting aspects of your performance that can be a weakness.

Goals will help you reach higher levels of personal performance. It will also help your coach in understanding what your inner goals are and how he or she can help you in your development.

Goal-setting is relevant to all aspects of your performance, technical, physical and mental as well as lifestyle.

Types of goals

There are two types of goals you can set:

*   **outcome** goals
*   **process** goals.

Outcome goals can be highly motivating and important to set, as they are concerned with the results or ambitions:

*   gaining selection
*   winning a medal
*   becoming top run-scorer.

These goals, however, are not always easy to control as they can be affected by the performance of others.

Process goals are about the detail – they relate to the "processes" you need to control if you are going to achieve your performance and outcome goals. Some examples would include:

- Passing accurately to my team-mate.

- Watching the ball at all times.

- Moving into space when I receive the ball.

- Including endurance sessions within training programme.

- Recording my results in fitness tests.

Process goals support your technical development in executing specific skills that are components of your overall performance. By establishing an effective foundation in your process goals, your performances will improve, which will have a desirable impact on the outcomes of your involvement.

Within your action plan, it is essential to consider the process goals and how they link to the outcome goals. There is little benefit in setting an outcome goal without considering what you need to do to get yourself performing in the way you wish to.

Depending on sources you use, you may see a third classification of goals – **performance goals**. These goals are linked to process goals, but more quantifiable, e.g. 75% success rate on tackles.

Be SMART

Toolkit: What is SMART?

SMART is the acronym for:

S _____

M _____

A _____

R _____

T _____

But what does it mean?

A simple guide to SMART

Specific: You need to be precise in stating your goals. Vague aims like "to improve success rates of my first serve" or "improve my fitness" are generally not very useful. A vague aim can be very difficult to measure and therefore it is difficult to see whether you have achieved them or not. . If you are more specific about what you are trying to achieve, you can establish exactly what you are trying to achieve. A more specific aim would be "to achieve a 75% success rate with my first serve". This is very specific as it means you need to focus training on your service. The fitness aim needs to be specific to one element of fitness. For example, this could be looking at measuring your endurance through bleep tests and or 12-minute runs.

Measurable: To be able to state where you are now you need to be able to measure your performance in some way. So, for our examples above you might measure heading effectiveness by testing your ability to complete a heading drill. You may need to be even more specific in looking at your accuracy over different distances and with different types of headers. Already you can see that thinking about measurement also helps you to be specific. It also means that you can probably identify the most important aspect of your heading to work on. So we might now state our goal as:

> "To improve my defensive heading accuracy 60% to 75% on the run and 80% to 90% when standing."

Achievable: Having stated a specific goal and decided how you will measure it, you need to check that it is realistic. Is it an improvement that you can work towards? Are there specific practices or training that you can do that will help? Ask a coach or team-mate if they think it's achievable. One of the things that successful athletes in all sports do is to set challenging goals that will be difficult to reach but that are controllable and within reach if you put in the necessary work.

Recorded: It's not really a goal until it's made formal and written down. By making the goal formal, you are more committed to doing it. Talking to team-mates, coaches and others about your goals is useful. If others are aware of what you are trying to achieve, they can support your efforts or observe your performances knowing what aspects they need to be watching. They can also share your achievements and the enjoyment of meeting your targets. If we look at the fitness example, you might decide that to improve endurance fitness from level 10 to level 11 on the bleep test (specific, measurable and achievable) you will run for 30 minutes 3 times a week. 'R' is also referred to as **realistic** depending on how SMART is interpreted.

Timescale: Finally, goals need to be set within a specific period of time. This is another great motivator and will spur you to action. Two examples of SMART goals might be:

1. To improve my defensive heading accuracy from 60% to 75% on the run and 80% to 90% when standing by the end of November.

2. To improve endurance fitness from level 10 to level 11 on the bleep test by the start of pre-season training.

Within your targets, you will need to consider who can support you in the process. This could be friends, parents, coaches, team-mates, doctor, physiotherapist and psychologist.

 Tutor talk

It is worth developing IT skills in Microsoft Excel for this aspect of your work, as it will help you in the production of graphs, charts and tables. Talk to IT support staff at your college to help you in this process. Graphs that have been professionally produced can support you in the quality of your assignment work.

Tutor talk

Talk to your tutor about your proposed targets. Take the time to write goals out in draft form and ask your tutor to check through to ensure that you have taken into account the SMART principles. The more you can work independently, the greater your opportunities to achieve a merit or distinction grade for the unit.

Milestones

A milestone is a mini-target that can be used to monitor your progress from starting your action plan to the targeted date for improvement. This monitoring process will enable you to assess whether you are making progress at the appropriate pace.

If, for example, you are not making the expected progress, you can increase the frequency and intensity of your practice to facilitate improvement. You can also change your targets if it transpires that you have achieved your goal well in advance of the target date.

Essentially, a milestone is a measure of progress towards the final destination.

Barriers

A barrier is simply something that may block or inhibit your progress towards your planned and targeted goal. Barriers can be quite general and have an impact on all areas of your training or be specific. A specific barrier will be unique to one particular area of your action plan. Barriers can be **internal**, as in relating to your own performance or **external**, relating to your circumstances.

An example of an **internal barrier** would be an injury.

An example of an **external barrier** would be mobility and travelling to training sessions.

Within **assessment activity 2** (see page 120) you will need to identify possible barriers and explain how you are to overcome them. You will also need to highlight alternative activities in the event of a barrier being raised. These alternative activities are known as **contingency** plans or procedures.

Toolkit: Potential action plan barriers

In class, discuss the potential barriers you will need to overcome during the period of time you are working on your action plan. Complete the spider diagram with the results of this discussion.

What barriers do you consider could prevent you from achieving your goal?

injury

ACTION PLAN BARRIERS

As part of your action plan, you will need to consider how you are going to overcome these barriers.

Drills, practises and observation points for matches, games and events

In order to achieve the progress that you plan to make during the time covered by your action plan, you will need to consider the types of activities you must complete.

These activities may include practices and drills to improve specific techniques and skills identified as weaknesses in your assessment of your current performance (Assessment activity 1). You can devise you own drills to support your development or you can access support from various personnel such as a coach or trainer, a physiotherapist, a doctor or even a sports psychologist.

You can also use sports specific and generic-coaching books, which will give you suggested drills. Please note that some drills can appear quite complex in diagrammatic form. It is always worth practising a drill before starting to record your progress. Taking this time to practise means that you have mastered the drill and can start to concentrate your efforts onto the development of the techniques.

If your action plan includes elements of your performance in matches and competitions where it may be difficult for you to record your progress, you will need to arrange for observations. Friends, peers, coaches, etc, can carry out observations. To record an observation, you will need to produce paperwork that is specific to the area of your performance being observed.

Finally, where possible, drills should look to develop from basic skills and techniques to more complex and realistic situations that simulate competition.

Assessment activity 2

Assessment activity 2 covers the following learning outcomes:

LO2:   Explore targets for future performance in a chosen sport

LO3:   Produce an effective performance plan taking into account barriers to achievement

The second assessment covers the production of an action/performance plan to develop the areas you have identified as weaknesses in the first assessment activity. For each area you will produce a SMART target and identify how you are going to improve from your current performance.

You must include detail on the types of internal and external barriers you are to overcome as you work towards your target.

Barriers will include:

- Injury
- Poor weather
- Resources
- Other activities

- Travel (mobility and transport)
- Team selection
- Lack of equipment
- Lack of coaching

- Part-time work
- College work
- Personal relationships
- Others

Finally, you will need to summarise the **SMART** targets and explain why these are important to you as a performer and how these improvements will help you. You can include details on the priority of certain targets over others.

 Author's advice

Be realistic about the number of areas on which you wish to concentrate your development onto. By prioritising in this way, you are working on the areas that will have the most significant impact on your performance.

Checklist

As with all assignment work, the following will be required:

	✓
Front cover	
Contents page	
Introduction	
Main text	
SMART target sheets	
Activity sheets (as required)	
Assignment sheet	
Bibliography	
Proof read	
Are all of your papers securely bound in a good quality wallet?	

Section 3: On reflection

LO4:   Monitor and evaluate performance

By the time you are working on *Section 3*, the main work of the unit has been completed. However, *Section 3* requires the most motivation. You will be working in and out of class on your action plan. This will include practical activities as well as filling in the necessary documentation to record your achievements on an ongoing basis.

Reflection in action

Schon (1987) identifies two types of reflection:

Reflection **IN** action

This is the process of thinking on your feet and responding accordingly.

Reflection **ON** action

This is the process of considering your performance after a match, competition, training, etc.

In the context of this unit, the reflection has started with the assessment of your current levels of performance. If you think back to the model of **Kolb's Learning Cycle** (see page 91), this underlines the experience, leading to reflection, leading to plans (your SMART targets) and performance again.

You will need to monitor your development towards your SMART targets and respond accordingly. This means that the reflection process is ongoing and not simply at the end of the timescales you have set for yourself. This is where **milestones** (see page 118) can be of most value.

To support this process, you will need to complete documentation of your experience as you complete the drills you have established. The completion of this documentation is the process of reflection in action. This completed documentation will form part of the evidence for the third and final assessment activity.

Methods to monitor and review progress

As mentioned above, the completion of documentation will assist you in the monitoring of your progress. However, you will also need to review this against your targets. As with your initial assessment, you can draw upon the expertise, experience and assistance of others, these typically being:

* your own thoughts and perceptions about your performance
* observations by your coach
* observations made by team-mates
* observations made by friends, parents and peers
* interviews with any of the above
* video analysis.

Most importantly, the results from your drills and practices will be the monitoring procedure. This process may involve the production of graphs to plot your progress.

A graph can be produced using Microsoft Excel and would look like the example below.

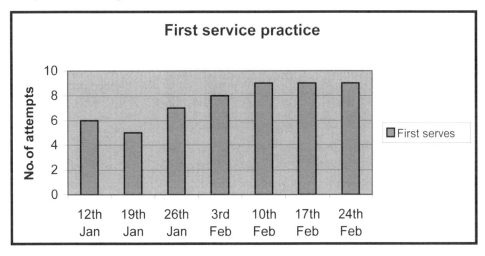

In this graph, you can see the date of the practice and the results achieved. Whilst this is a relatively simple graph analysing a simple drill, you can start to add conditions. For example, if you were a tennis player experiencing difficulties in holding your service games, it would be prudent to work on first serves and avoiding double faults (especially, if this was the main cause of not holding your service games in competitions).

If this was the case, then the graph can be made more complex. Using the same dates you can start to analyse the results looking at the occurrences of double faults when practising serving. By producing graphs, you are able to plot your progress visually and see trends (upwards or otherwise) quickly. Within *assignment activity 3* you will need to explain why certain results were recorded.

From the second graph you are able to see that by the 6th practice session, no double faults have been recorded.

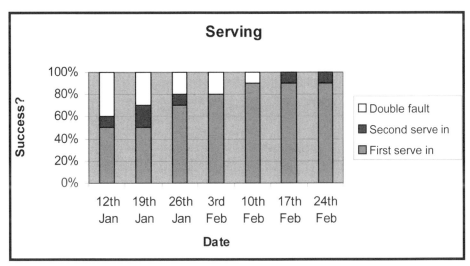

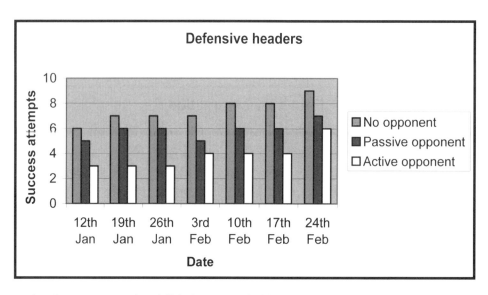

Another example of a more complex drill being recorded in a graph would be as follows. If you were a defender in football and you were concerned about your headed clearances, then you may have three separate drills to record your progress:

Drill 1 – Heading (no opponents)

Drill 2 – Heading (passive opponent)

Drill 3 – Heading (active opponent)

The graph produced is easy to analyse and you can plot the progress towards your intended target. You can submit ongoing graphs and charts, match observations, witness statements, etc, with your **Progress Review** documentation.

Your progress will be monitored during tutorials and you will have time in class to practice the drills you wish to use to facilitate your development.

 Author's advice

It is worth developing skills using Excel to support the production of graphs. If you're unsure about how to produce graphs, **ASK!**

You will decide how you wish to monitor your progress.

Assessment activity 3

Assessment activity 3 covers the following learning outcome:

LO4: Monitor and evaluate performance

The purpose of this final assessment activity is to carry out all the proposed drills and practices planned in the SMART targets. You will also propose new drills as you monitor your performance against your expected levels.

You will produce graphs, witness testimonies, self-assessment reports and any other evidence of your performance. You will need to evaluate the drills and your progress on a regular basis. These evaluations will be based on the milestones you have set within your action plan.

What is an evaluation?

In a nutshell, an **evaluation** is part of the monitoring process where you look at the development that has taken place. For example, if your aim was to improve first-serve accuracy from 35% to 70% in four months, you may aim for steady progress each month. Alternatively, you may aim for early progress, then a plateau followed by another period of improvement (see graph below).

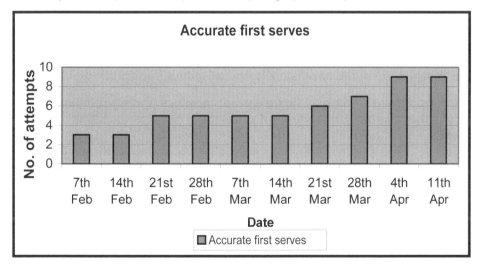

If you evaluate your progress over these weeks, you will see in weeks 3 to 6 (21st February to 14th March) that improvement remained at 50% accuracy. In your evaluation you would need to explain why this plateau was experienced and what was done to support the improvement seen in weeks 7, 8, 9 and 10.

Within your evaluation, you would also mention support and guidance received from coaches, peers, physiotherapists, etc.

Where necessary, your evaluation will include details of how you have had to modify your action plan in response to unexpected progress (in terms of over- and under-achievement!). You will also detail any unforeseen barriers that inhibited your progress.

What do I actually submit?

- Completed review documentation (**Action Plan Review**).

- **Graphs** highlighting progress with evaluative comments included.

- **Observation forms** (match forms highlighting specific areas in your performance that are part of your action plan, e.g. number of successful defensive headers in a match against the number of unsuccessful ones).

- **Feedback** from others and yourself about your performance.

- A **summary evaluation** of progress on each target (this will need to be one of the last pieces of work to be written prior to submission) that concludes the results achieved throughout the action plan.

- A **final summary** of the whole action plan and **proposals** for future performances (the final detail to be written!).

Author's advice

As highlighted, *assessment activity 3* consists of mini-assessments, one for each SMART target. It is suggested that you treat it as such and that you have separate plastic wallets for each target and only bring it together a few days before submitting to work for final assessment.

You will use the tutorials to obtain feedback about your performance. This can come from the subject lecturer or from classmates. You will have tutorials in small groups to support this.

Example documentation to help you in all the assessment activities is available from the website, **www.lexden-publishing.co.uk/btecsport**. You can use these forms as you see fit and customise them for your own needs.

Author's advice

Reflective Practitioner requires constant effort over the year rather than a bit here and there. As such, it is not the type of project that can be put down and forgotten about. It will need you to complete a little each week. Whenever you are involved in training or competition, either formal or informal, it can be reflected upon as evidence for your assessment activities. By following this little and often process, it can be completed quickly and effectively. The overall aim of this unit is to support your progress in your sport, as well as being part of the course you need to pass. The big benefit is that you don't have to spend hours completing research or finding specific facts, but that is not to say this is an easy option. I hope that this book makes the unit less complex and that it supports you and your efforts, both in terms of sports and academic performance.

Contents

Unit 3: Ethics and Values in Sport

Introduction to the unit

Unit 3: Ethics and Values in Sport is a compulsory unit of the National Certificate/Diploma in Sport. It is closely linked to **Unit 1: Sport in Society**.

This unit will introduce you to moral and ethical issues in sport and how to deal with these effectively in the work environment.

You will learn about the key principles, ethics and values underpinning sport and the effect that good or bad conduct of participants, coaches officials and spectators can have on the image of a sport and all the people involved in it.

You will learn to understand the importance that national and international sport governing bodies place on ethical codes and good practice, and the role they have in implementing them.

Through discussion of topical issues and your own fact finding, you will recognise the positive influence sport can have in education and personal development, and how this influence can translate into other aspects of later life.

Aims of the unit

This unit is aimed at developing your understanding of principles, ethics, values and standards associated with sport. It will enable you to appreciate the important role sport can play in developing individuals in society and how it can act as a reflection of the fundamental ethics and values that are formed.

This unit will help you appreciate the standards, ethics and values that underpin sport. You will learn about the roles, responsibilities and behaviour expected of participants (professionals and non-professionals), coaches and managers, officials, volunteers and spectators. At the end of this unit, you will be able to explain the core principles, ethics and values associated with sport, identify good practice and devise a code of conduct for a chosen sport.

You will be able to include ethics and values in lesson plans for sporting activities and ensure their implementation.

The ultimate aim of this unit is to ensure you appreciate that ethics and values form the basis of sport in society, and how important it is that you as a sporting practitioner integrate them into your everyday work.

What the content will cover

This unit has many links with **Unit 1: Sport in Society** and enables you to draw on the knowledge gained from that unit.

Initially, you will be introduced to definitions of principles, ethics, values and standards and how they are associated with sport. You will look at various sports governing bodies and other organisations involved in sport, and how they apply and implement ethics and values.

You will discuss the benefits of committing to ethics and values, for individuals and organisations, and the consequences of ignoring them.

Based on the above, you will learn about the positive impact sport and its ethical framework can have on the development of individuals in a physical as well as mental sense.

This will enable you to investigate ethics and values across a range of sports situations. Current major sporting events will provide you with plenty of material to discuss topic issues.

You will look at codes of practice and behaviour developed by sporting organisations and how they implement these codes. Then you will have the opportunity to develop your own code for a chosen sport/facility/activity.

Lastly, there will be a "hands on" exercise. Drawing on what you have learned so far, you will plan, deliver and evaluate two sporting activities for which you must identify the relevant principles, ethics and values.

What will I do in class?

Class sessions will provide you with the necessary forum to explore the many and various ethical issues in modern sport.

Formal input by your tutor will give you a good platform from which you can start your own fact finding and research.

There are quite a few websites with interesting material relevant to the learning outcomes you have to meet. For example, most governing bodies of major sports have developed their own code of conduct, there are value statements published for NVQs in sport, and there are several sites dealing with drugs, corruption and child protection issues.

This unit allows you to delve into a range of sports situation and debate current ethical issues. You should follow the media regarding any such issues and bring them up for discussion in class; this will help your tutor to keep this unit highly topical.

You also will be involved in the practical side. Learning outcome 4 (and usually one task in the IVA) requires you to plan, carry out and evaluate at least two different sporting activities, implementing ethics and values relevant to the selected sports. You will need some time in class to organise these practical sessions. Your tutor may have to help you with identifying an appropriate venue and group such as a local school or club.

How will I be assessed?

Ethics and Values in Sport is assessed together with **Unit 1: Sport in Society** via an externally-set assignment that cover both these units. This is called the **Integrated Vocational Assessment** (IVA). Your tutor will obtain this assignment from BTEC and then pass it on to you (see Unit 1). Please note that the IVA constitutes a double unit; therefore the grade achieved in it counts for two units.

The Ethics and Values unit is made up of four Learning Outcomes (LO):

LO1:   **Explore the principles, values and ethics associated with sport**

LO2:   **Investigate values and ethics in a range of sports situations**

LO3:   **Propose a code of practice for use in a chosen sports facility or activity**

LO4:   **Plan an activity using principles, ethics and values appropriate to the selected sports activity**

You will have a variety of tasks to complete that build up towards the final assessment; each of these tasks will be linked to the Learning Outcomes and the grading criteria.

What are ethics and values in sport?

Ethics and values have always played an important role in sport. In **Unit 1: Sport in Society**, you identified the main characteristics of sport as being **competitive**, involving **physical activity** and **bound by rules**. Sport is about **competition**, and competition is about **winning**. You will be familiar with concepts like **fair play** and **playing within the rules** or **being a good sport**. The reason why we have rules and officials is to ensure that every participant competes on a level playing field and rules are applied impartially. The basic idea of any sporting competition is that the best athlete or team wins.

However, in reality, this is not always the case. Throughout history, sport has been used as a political pawn – for instance the boycott of the Olympic Games in Moscow in 1980 by the USA and the retaliating boycott of the 1984 games in Los Angeles by the Warsaw Pact countries. Hitler used the 1936 games in Berlin to portray the power of National Socialism and the "Aryan Master Race", and during the period of the Cold War, Communist East and Capitalistic West used the games to demonstrate the superiority of their political systems. Even in ancient Greece and Rome sport and games were often used to further political careers.

When the England team won the football World Cup in 1966, each player received £500 and a coat (they could choose from either white or beige). Nowadays though, sport is big business, and the money involved is counted in tens of millions of pounds. Top sportspersons earn seven-figure salaries, they gain celebrity status and there are lucrative sponsorship deals involved. The winning or losing of a match or competition can mean the difference between good profits or insolvency. For football clubs, promotion to the Premier League is synonymous with more money; relegation can spell financial disaster (e.g. Bradford City, Nottingham Forrest and Leeds United).

The difference between a gold and silver medal can mean millions of pounds because of advertising and sponsorship deals; in tennis, the difference between winning a major tournament and being the runner up is a six-figure number.

Because of the high stakes involved, there is tremendous pressure on athletes to win at all costs, and often people are prepared to bend, or even break, the rules to win. Performance-enhancing drugs is just one example of rule breaking, match fixing and bribery another. As a result, high performance sport has received a lot of bad publicity in the last few years.

This has led to great concern about ethical issues in sport not only among sports-related organisations, but also in society in general. Administrators and the majority of fans are worried about a decline in standards of sporting conduct such as lack of respect for officials and rules, incidents of gamesmanship, cheating, doping, child abuse and spectator violence. Recently, it has been mentioned that live football should be televised after the 9pm watershed because of the influence of poor player behaviour on youngsters.

As *Schembri, G. and Steffen, C. (1999): The Ethical Challenge Facing Sport, Australian Sports Commission*, rightly argue:

> *"For sport to lose its value as something worth honouring would be to diminish it as an agent of social cohesion. Sport as a source of role models would be lost and sport as an activity of joy and pleasure would be diminished."*

Of course, sport can contribute very positively to the development of individuals, on a personal as well as social level. Sport is a great way to channel energy, build confidence, gain achievement (physically and mentally) – it should transcend the boundaries of social class and race and religion. It can teach acceptance of rules and self-discipline, and the benefits of teamwork. You can experience the joy of success, and learn to recognise excellence, at whatever level. Top sportspersons often act as role models for young people.

Sport should improve fitness levels, contribute to a healthy lifestyle and enhance the quality of life. It can provide a stimulating environment in which to socialise and enjoy a personal challenge.

The London Declaration on Expectations for Fairness in Sport (2001) states that:

> *"…ethically-based and safe sport promotes an active lifestyle, self-esteem, healthy bodies, lifelong learning and strong team spirit."*

As you can see, sport can have both positive and negative influences and impacts. Therefore, be it as a sports practitioner, a coach, an administrator, an official or an athlete, you should be aware of the ethical issues in sport.

As you know from the **Sport in Society** unit, sport does not exist in a vacuum, but has been socially constructed, i.e. it is part of society and as such not only shares in its values and beliefs, but represents them. Just think about the racial abuse black England players suffered during the friendly football match against Spain in November 2004 and the repercussions of this spectator behaviour. What has this done to the image of Spanish society, Spanish football and football in general?

Section 1: The good···The bad···The ugly

LO1: Explore the principles, values and ethics associated with sport.

A negative view of sport

The famous writer George Orwell (he wrote the highly acclaimed novel *1984*) wrote in the *Sporting Spirit* in 1945:

"Serious sport has nothing to do with fair play. It is bound up with hatred, jealousy, boastfulness, and disregard of all rules and sadistic pleasure in witnessing violence; in other words it is war minus the shooting."

 Toolkit: Sporting spirit

1. Do you think that Orwell would have such a negative view of sport today (he wrote the above statement in 1945)?

2. Draft a short reply to George Orwell, explaining, with examples if possible, why you think he is wrong (or right).

What are we talking about?

Before we go on, it is important that you are clear about the terminology. The words, **ethics**, **values**, **principles**, **morals**, and **standards** are often used interchangeably although, strictly speaking, they have clear definitions.

 Toolkit: Defining terminology

Refer to a dictionary and define the following words (note that princip**le** should not to be confused with princip**al**, ethics should not to be confused with eth**n**ic).

Principles: _____

Ethics: _____

Values: _____

Standards: _____

Morals: _____

Toolkit: Terminology in a sporting context

Having found the definitions for the different terms, now see if you can apply them in a sports context by either thinking of an example or, even better, of a real case. The examples can be good or bad.

Tip: There were plenty of examples during the 2004 Olympics.

Term	Example
Principles	
Ethics	
Values	e.g. It is wrong to take performance-enhancing drugs to seek victory.
Moral behaviours	
Standards	

Sportsmanship v. Gamesmanship

In thc context of ethical behaviour, people often talk about sportsmanship and gamesmanship. Sometimes, people get these terms confused, or they assume they both mean the same. This is not the case.

⚒ Toolkit: Definition of sportsmanship and gamesmanship

What do you think sportsmanship and gamesmanship mean? Give your own definition!

Sportsmanship is _____

Gamesmanship is _____

_____

_____

Now compare your definition with those of your fellow students. Now try and think of a real life example from the world of sport for sportsmanship and gamesmanship. Complete the table after your discussions.

Example of gamesmanship:

Why was this gamesmanship?

Example of sportsmanship:

Why was this sportsmanship?

Benefits of ethics and values

The importance of ethics and values is to ensure the positive effects of sport on the individual and, consequently, on the community. Sport is a subsystem of society and therefore all people involved in it have a responsibility to safeguard the ethics and values that underpin a well-functioning society by promoting these in a sporting context. Even as a purely recreational activity, acceptance of rules, respect for officials and opponents and fair play are necessary for sport to fulfil this basic function. In a wider, competitive and international context, sport portrays the importance a society ascribes to certain principles and values. Sportsman-like or unsportsman-like behaviour of athletes, spectators and managers can often reflect on the country as a whole in line with the pressure placed on winning at all costs.

Toolkit: Manager's behaviour

The UEFA referee Anders Frisk was subjected to threats against him and his family after the Chelsea manager Jose Mourinho launched his verbal attack on him after the 1st leg of a Champions League fixture against Barcelona. This led Frisk to resign as an international referee after a 26-year career as a referee.

In a group, discuss what you feel this says about the state of professional football today?

Positive and negative experience

By applying ethics and values, principles and high standards, not just the individual, but also the sporting organisation benefits.

The benefits of sport for an individual and its character-building potential have long been recognised. The ancient Greeks placed great importance on sport as part of the overall education of young people.

The way sport is handled and managed by the people in charge can lead to positive and negative experiences for participants. Most of us get enjoyment and a sense of achievement out of sport, but others can be put off sport for life through negative experiences.

Toolkit: The consequences of ethics and values

Read the two case studies on the following pages. Identify the benefits and consequences of having good or bad ethics and values for:

- each club
- the participants
- the local community.

Complete the table at the end of the scenarios.

Case study: Club A

This youth football team has a very enthusiastic and ambitious new coach who is desperate for promotion.

He puts enormous pressure on the team members to win at all costs and actively encourages gamesmanship – stretching the rules and trying to get away with bending them in order to win. He actively encourages hard physical contact during matches to "take out" good players of the opposition.

During training sessions, he gives a lot of time and attention to the better players and is prone to running down the weaker players with sarcastic comments. He uses a lot of foul and obscene language in the training sessions and during matches. He tends to ignore the two black players in the team completely and despite being good players, uses them only as substitutes.

He also argues openly with parents and during matches hurls abuse at the referee, for which he has already received a touchline ban. When the team lost the last match, the coach shouted and swore at the youngsters in the changing rooms, calling them names.

On occasions, he has pushed the youngsters too hard, resulting in severe lactic acidosis and, in two cases, injuries.

As a result of the coach's behaviour, the club secretary has received several complaints from parents, and two parents have already withdrawn their children from the club.

The club is already struggling with membership numbers and relies on a certain number for funding from the local sports council.

	Participant	Club	Local community
Benefits			
Consequences			

Case study : Club B

This club plays in the same league as Club A. Its coach, too, is very competitive and wants promotion for the team but applies a different approach to achieve his goal.

He uses positive feedback to get the best out of his players and when he criticises , he does it in a positive, constructive manner without belittling the player. He gives every player, even the not so good ones, an equal amount of time and attention. He encourages respect for the opponents and match officials; if he does not agree with the referee, he talks to him in private after the match.

He works his players hard during training sessions, but does not push them beyond their limits. He takes time to listen to the youngsters' problems and treats everything they tell him in strictest confidence.

He talks to his players about the importance of team work and team spirit and its importance for the success of the team. As a result, all players in the team have become good friends, and the team has bonded well together, which allows everybody to play to his strengths.

On one occasion, an over-ambitious parent interfered with the training session – the coach asked him politely to speak to him afterwards.

The coach's language is always positive and encouraging, and the youngsters respond well to it.

He discourages gamesmanship such as diving in the penalty area and arguing with the referee. When one of his players abused the referee, the coach asked to see him after the match and talked to him about why his behaviour was wrong.

After a defeat, the coach still praises the players' efforts, then he analyses the match with the players and uses the defeat as a learning experience.

He constantly explains the importance of a healthy life style.

The club has become very popular and receives a lot of support from its local community.

	Participant	Club	Local community
Benefits			
Consequences			

Toolkit: Positive influences

What positive influences does sport have on you?

Positive influences of sport

self esteem

Toolkit: Positive and negative values associated with sport

Not all values associated with sport are positive. Using the table below, note the positive and negative experiences that can be associated with your own sport. Try and think how this can affect the everyday life of the individual having these experiences.

Positive values	Effect on individual	Negative values	Effect on individual
E.g. team work	Learns to put the team before the individual.	Cheating to win is OK.	Loss of sense of achievement.

The importance of ethics and values for young people in sport

One of the most important aspects of ethics and values is that children, if taught early enough, will take them on board and make them their own. Good behaviour, high standards and awareness of ethical issues absorbed by children in a sporting environment can be transferred into daily life and help shape their character and views and vice versa, moral standards and values learned in day-to-day life by children will be transferred into sport.

A survey on public opinion on youth and sport carried out in Canada in 2002 showed that the most serious problems facing youngsters in sport were seen to be:

- overemphasis on winning and competition
- too much or too little parental involvement
- violence, drugs and harassment – but to a lesser extent.

The study also found that involvement in community sport appeared to create a more positive attitude towards the contribution of sport to youth values and how sport benefits the broader community. (Source: *Decima Research (2002): Canadian Public Opinion Survey on Youth and Sport – Report prepared for Canadian Centre for Ethics in Sport.*)

 ## Toolkit: Examining the consequences of winning at all costs

In groups of two or three, or individually, note in bullet point format your responses to the following:

1. What, in your view, creates the overemphasis on winning and competition? Explain what the consequences of this "win at all cost" pressure could have for youths, and how it could shape their values.

2. Why does involvement in community sports create more positive values, and how can this benefit the whole community?

How would I like to be treated?

Relationships between human beings are based on principles, ethics and values. These relationships can take many forms, from relationships between two individuals to relationships between large groups in society and whole nations.

Within the context of sports, a variety of these relationships exist, including the following:

- Relationships between people on the same level of authority or influence (e.g. players in a team or employees in a sports centre).

- Relationships between people of different levels of authority or influence (e.g. coach and the team, sports centre management and its staff).

- Relationships between service providers and service recipients (e.g. a local authority holiday activity scheme and its customers).

- Relationships between volunteers and their organisation.

- Relationships between children and persons in charge of them. This position of a person entrusted by parents with their child is called *in loco parentis*; it means "in the place of parents", and it carries great legal responsibility.

These relationships involve principles and values such as honouring trust, responsibility, confidentiality, mutual respect, acknowledgement of achievement, health and safety, regard for the law, loyalty, well being of staff/clients/participants, fairness, considerations of participants/employees' needs, humanity and dignity, etc.

It is important to adhere to these often unwritten principles because if disregarded, people in these relationships will feel cheated, hurt and/or betrayed.

For instance, imagine, you have just told your coach in confidence the reason that you have been underperforming lately is because your partner had "dumped" you for someone else. Later on, when you meet in the pub after the training session, you find out that your coach has told all your team-mates about your partner leaving you, and you become the butt of everybody's joke.

How would you feel about your coach? Would you confide in him or her again?

Toolkit: Disregarding principles and ethics

Scenario 1

Mrs Rantandrave has enrolled her eight-year-old daughter, Lucy, in the local council's summer holiday play scheme at the park.

On the first day, she drops Lucy off at ten o'clock in the morning. When she comes back at four o'clock in the afternoon to pick up Lucy, the play scheme supervisor can't find her. There does not appear to be a list of children on the scheme. Mrs Rantandrave notices quite a lot of children running around in the large park, totally unsupervised. She finally finds Lucy walking along the main road adjacent to the park with a couple of other children. She takes Lucy home and decides to withdraw her from the play scheme. The next day, Mrs Rantandrave demands to see the council officer in charge of the holiday scheme and files a formal complaint.

Task

Unfortunately, Mrs Rantandrave is not very good at formal letters. You have to help her. Formulate a letter of complaint to the local authority, explaining what principles, ethics and values have been breached by not supervising her daughter, Lucy, properly.

Scenario 2

You are the assistant sports development officer in your local authority. You thought very hard about increasing the participation rate of youngster during the holiday activity schemes and came up with some really good ideas.

You tell your line manager, Mr Creep, about these ideas so he can discuss them with the department manager.

A week later, when you meet the head of department in the canteen, he mentions Mr Creep's fantastic ideas for the holiday schemes. You realise that your line manager has passed your ideas for his and has taken all the credit.

Later on that day, you see Mr Creep in the office. You decide to confront him.

Role play

One of the other students can play Mr Creep.

Work out what you would say to Mr Creep. Confront him with the relevant principles and ethics that he has disregarded.

Mr Creep is allowed to defend himself by questioning these principles and ethics.

Section 2: Winning at all costs?

LO2:   Investigate values and ethics in a range of sports situations

In modern elite sport, there is a lot of pressure for top class athletes to win at all costs because of the money, status and also their short careers. These pressures have tempted some coaches, managers and athletes to cheat and justify their actions by overemphasising the importance of victory. Such behaviour has undermined the basic principles of fair play and competing within the rules. Perhaps the most famous advocate of this was the American football coach, Vince Lombardi, who famously said:

"Winning is not the most important thing, it is the only thing."

 Toolkit: Defending the indefensible

Debate the following statement:

"Winning at all costs is perfectly acceptable in modern sport."

Argument for the statement	Argument against the statement

Why are there different ethics and values in different sports?

Most sports have a certain image that is based on the good or bad things we associate with it. These in turn are based on the way participants and spectators behave, and what code of conduct they are expected to follow.

Toolkit: Match sports to their positive or negative perceptions

Match the sports listed below to the positive or negative perceptions associated with them.

Sports: tennis, boxing, golf, cricket, horse racing, weightlifting, snooker, athletics, motor racing, rowing…and any other sports you think are appropriate.

Association	Sports
Aggression	e.g. *boxing*
Violence	
Cheating and bending the rules	
Corruption and tampering	
Fixing of results	
Doping	
Racism	
Hooliganism	
Sporting behaviour	
Honesty and respect	
Owning up to mistakes and fouls	
Teamwork	
Loyalty and commitment	

When you analyse the reasons you have matched certain sports with particular associations, you'll find that this is probably because of a number of factors such as:

- nature of the sport
- social status of the sport participants
- background of spectators
- history of the sport
- money involved
- pressure from fans and media
- level at which sport is played.

Some of these factors you have already addressed in **Unit 1: Sport in Society**.

Ethics and values in contrasting sports

There are general principles, ethics and values that traditionally applied to all sports – such as fairness, abiding by the rules and impartiality of officials – but others vary according to the individual sport.

For example, arguing with the referee is almost commonly accepted in football; in rugby such behaviour would not be tolerated.

 Toolkit: Analysing ethics and values in contrasting sports

Analyse these two contrasting sports: professional golf and professional football. Consider the characteristics that are commonly seen in these sports.

1. Complete the following by rating the characteristics below for the two sports 1–5 (1 rarely seen and 5 means very often seen).

Characteristics	Golf rating					Football rating				
Gentlemanly behaviour	1	2	3	4	5	1	2	3	4	5
Fair play	1	2	3	4	5	1	2	3	4	5
Gamesmanship	1	2	3	4	5	1	2	3	4	5
Cheating	1	2	3	4	5	1	2	3	4	5
Abuse of official	1	2	3	4	5	1	2	3	4	5
Taunting of opposition	1	2	3	4	5	1	2	3	4	5
Spectator misbehaviour	1	2	3	4	5	1	2	3	4	5
Respect for the values of the game	1	2	3	4	5	1	2	3	4	5
Score for positive characteristics										
Score for negative characteristics										

2. From the above list, identify the scores for positive behaviours, (i.e. those that society considers desirable) and negative behaviour, (i.e. those that society considers undesirable). Provide an explanation for the differences between the two sports.

As can been seen from your table, ethics and values in particular sports differ greatly. A team sport may differ from an individual sport in respect of the underpinning values. For example, playing football requires an emphasis on team cohesion and team spirit.

Toolkit: Comparing ethics and values in contrasting sports

Compare different and contrasting sports and the particular ethics and values associated with them.

Examine:

- contact sport v. non-contact sport (e.g. boxing v. tennis)
- sport involving technical equipment v. sport not involving technical
- equipment (e.g. running v. motor racing)
- sport in which the result is judgement based v. sports in which results are factual and absolute (e.g. figure skating v. 100m sprint)
- highly physical sports v. highly skill-based sports (e.g. marathon running v. snooker).

Author's advice

Most sports have developed guidelines on accepted behaviour whilst participating in their sport. These are often referred to as codes of conduct. Check out the Royal and Ancient (R&A) (**www.randa.org**) for golf, the Football Association (FA) (**www.thefa.com**) and the International Olympic Committee (IOC) (**www.olympic.org**) websites for codes of conduct or behaviour.

Toolkit: Examining the ethical behaviour of players

Read the following case study:

Case study

In January 2005, during the dying minutes of the Premier League match between Tottenham Hotspurs and Manchester United, the Manchester goalkeeper failed to stop a long shot properly. The keeper reacted quickly; he dived after the ball and "fished" it out just as it had crossed the goal line. The referee was not able to see the situation properly and decided it was not a goal. As a result, the game was a draw and Tottenham lost two points.

There was a heated debate within the football fraternity and amongst sports journalists and fans as to whether the goalkeeper should have "owned up": some argued he had acted correctly, others accused him of cheating.

Discuss this in small groups and record the points made; then present them to the class.

Then, individually, write a letter to a newspaper explaining why, in your view, the goalkeeper acted ethically or not.

It's not fair

In **Unit 1: Sport in Society**, you may have discussed the characteristics of modern sport. One of these characteristics is **equal opportunities**. It is generally recognised that some inequalities in sport still exist and **Sport England** (**www.sportengland.org.uk**) has acknowledged this and developed an equity statement.

Historically, participation and administration in sport has been dominated by white, middle class males. Just imagine, after the 1928 Olympics, long and middle-distance running for women was taken off the programme because it was deemed unfeminine to cross the finish line panting and sweating and with faces distorted with effort. It was not until 1984 that women were allowed to compete in the marathon at the Olympic Games.

Tutor talk

Talk with your tutor about what is meant by **equity** and by **prejudices**.

Toolkit: Defining equity and prejudice

From you discussion, provide a definition of the following terms:

Equity is: _____

Prejudice is: _____

Toolkit: Examining equitable and prejudiced behaviour

Read through the four short scenarios on the following pages about coaching and discuss within your group whether they are examples of equitable or prejudiced behaviour and why.

Scenario 1

Whilst you are coaching a group of young boys at soccer, you hear one of the coaches telling the boys within his group that they are useless and that they play like girls.

Equitable or prejudiced behaviour?

Reasons why:

Scenario 2

A young swimmer with special needs has been training for over 12 months for the Special Olympics. He attends for training on a daily basis an Adult Training Centre where there is a swimming pool. The local authority has decided as part of a cost-cutting exercise that it will no longer bus the swimmer the 12 miles he has to travel to the centre and has withdrawn him from the Centre without discussing the problem. He has been placed in another Training Centre that does not have a pool and he is now unable to train.

Equitable or prejudiced behaviour?

Reasons why:

Scenario 3

A young girl soccer player has been playing Sunday League football in her twin brother's U10s football side. She is very skilful and fully worthy of her place in the side. The secretary of the league has written to the coach saying that she will no longer be able to play for the side because she is a girl and the changing facilities are inadequate.

Equitable or prejudiced behaviour?

Reasons why:

Strategies for dealing with it:

Scenario 4

A talented, young Asian rugby player, Amir, has just joined a local rugby team where he is the only ethnic minority member. Despite his obvious abilities, he has not been well integrated into the squad. He has the potential to be in the 1st XV, but the club coach is reluctant to select him because he feels it would have a detrimental effect on the team spirit he has generated. After training, Amir feels he is unwelcome when socialising in the club house.

Equitable or prejudiced behaviour?

Reasons why:

Strategies for dealing with it:

It's against the law

Equity should be one of the basic principles of modern society, and it has also become one of the cornerstones of modern sport. No one wishing to participate in sport should be discriminated against on the basis of his/her race, colour, religion, class or cultural background, or because of a disability. To refuse anyone on those grounds would be considered contravening basic human rights and insulting a person's dignity.

Indeed, one of the major social roles of sport is that of an **equaliser**. People are judged on their performance, ability and skill, not on the colour of their skin or race.

In Great Britain, and Europe, **equality** is enforced by **equality legislation**, which makes discrimination illegal. The **Equal Opportunities Commission** (**EOC**) is the body that oversees equality. Its website is **www.eoc.org.uk**.

 Toolkit: Investigating equality legislation

Provide information on the following equality legislation:

Equality aspect	Legislation	What does it say?
Sex discrimination		
Disability		
Race		
Religion/culture		
Equal pay		

Toolkit: An equity training day

You are to prepare an equity training day for volunteer helpers at a festival of sport that is being held at your local sports centre. This festival will include coaching sessions, competitions and taster sessions for children.

In small groups select one of the following topics:

- safety
- racism
- gender
- disability
- child protection
- equal opportunities for all.

Then:

1. Create your own sport-related case study that identifies the relevant ethics and values you consider important.

2. Create your own training package for these and explain how to deal with these issues.

Section 3: Be on your best behaviour

This section covers learning outcome 3 and part of learning outcome 1.

LO1   Explore the principles, values and ethics associated with sport (principles and ethics)

LO3   Propose a code of practice for use in a chosen sports facility or activity

Principles, standards and ethical behaviour

People who work in the sports and leisure industry are expected to abide by certain principles and behave in an ethical way. Of course, principles, standards and ethics apply to all employment sectors; some are general, others are more specific.

For example, a general standard would be **safe practices at work** – in fact, it is governed by legislation. This is relevant to all work sectors.

A more specific standard for someone, say, working as a personal trainer would be a **healthy lifestyle**. This would not necessarily apply to a pub landlord or lorry driver.

Toolkit: Matching standards and ethical behaviour to particular jobs

A number of principles, standards and ethical behaviours are listed below. Match these to the particular jobs listed in the table. Mark the general ones (i.e. ones you think apply to all work sectors) with a **G** and the specific ones (i.e. only relevant to the particular job) with an **S**. Note: You can have more than one principle and ethical behaviour in a box!

Proper attire, confidentiality, integrity, trust, health and safety, responsibility for clients, treat all participants fairly, equality, healthy lifestyle, respect, personal hygiene, sportsmanship, social inclusion, treat people with dignity, making clients feel welcome, keeping fit, politeness and courtesy, being a team player, law abiding, personal standards, disabled access.

Job	Principles, standards, ethical behaviour	General (G) Specific (S)
Health Club Manager		
Children's Activity Supervisor		
Sports Centre Receptionist		
Gymnastic Coach		
Lifeguard		
Sailing Instructor		
Sport Therapist		
Sport Development Officer		
Community Sports Co-ordinator		

It is very important for employees to adhere to the principles and ethics of their organisations because the represent the ethos of their organisation. **Ethos** means the underpinning belief system and culture of an organisation.

Toolkit: Principles, standards and ethical behaviour role play

Scenario

Fred has just started his first job after leaving school on a Modern Apprenticeship scheme in a large local authority leisure centre. As leisure assistant, he is involved in the day-to-day running of the centre such as setting up the sports hall, getting equipment ready, cleaning, occasional reception duties and helping out in the popular After School Activity Programme for eight- to 12-year-olds.

Fred, however, has not quite grasped the importance of correct standards and the ethical behaviour required of him. He often ignores the girls in the group and lets the boys play football.

He chews gum when supervising the children's sports activities, and often he joins in and shows off. Fred also thinks that cleaning the sports hall is boring, and therefore doesn't do it properly. As a result, a badminton player slipped and fell on a piece of glass left over from the last computer fair in the hall.

When on lifeguard duty, Fred often does not to stick to his position and often chats to other lifeguards and customers, not paying due attention to his duty. When young girls are in the pool, Fred tends to show off.

Fred sometimes hides outside the back of the centre where he smokes in view of the public; his personal appearance leaves a lot to desire, and he often makes inappropriate jokes when on reception duty. Fred also thinks it's "cool" to walk round with his uniform T-shirt hanging out and his trainers' laces not tied.

The leisure centre policy is that staff can use the facilities for free as they are available on a stand-by basis. Staff cannot pre-book without paying. Fred, however, abused his privilege and booked himself and a friend onto a squash court at peak time. Unfortunately for him, he was found out and was called into the manager's office.

Role play

One student to play Fred, the other the manager.

In view of Fred's misconduct and general attitude, his manager has decided to give him some "advice" as to what conduct is expected of him. Explain to Fred the **principles** and **ethics** of his job, what **behaviour** is required of him, and why!

Impact of principles, standards and ethical behaviour

As discussed in the previous Toolkit, having high ethics and values in sport can have a number of positive impacts on the individual and the organisation. Conversely, the absence of ethics and values can have many negative impacts. It is therefore important for individuals and organisations to assess and evaluate these impacts.

Most individuals assess the impacts of their ethical behaviour informally, almost subconsciously. They "know" what is right or wrong through their upbringing, which in turn is determined by the principles, ethics and values of parents, peer group, society and a number of other influences such as the media.

Toolkit: Examine your behaviour and its impact

In the diagram below note the impacts your principles and ethics can have on the world around you.

Impacts of my ethical behaviour on my immediate world

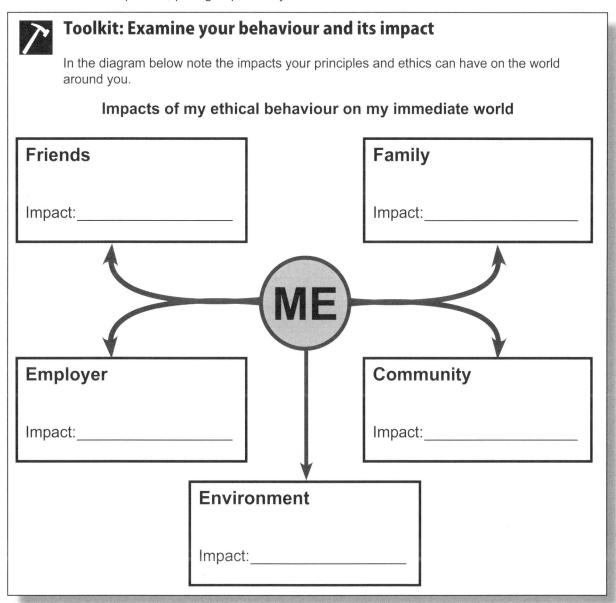

Friends		Family
Impact:_____		Impact:_____

ME

Employer		Community
Impact:_____		Impact:_____

Environment

Impact:_____

Standards, principles and ethics of sports organisations

Like individuals, organisations have to act ethically if they do not want to create a negative impact on the world around them. Often, the demand for profits pushes business to the edge of what is ethically acceptable, and beyond. It is the business equivalent of "winning at all cost".

Toolkit: The impact of principles and ethics of an organisation's stakeholders

In groups discuss the impact of principles and ethics of an organisation on its **stakeholders**. Complete the diagram below.

Remember there are several aspects to this. These include people working in the organisation, its customers and the local community. These groups are often referred to as **stakeholders**. These principles and ethics also impact on the way the business operates.

For example, approaching the player of another football club outside the transfer window and without permission of that club is generally considered unethical.

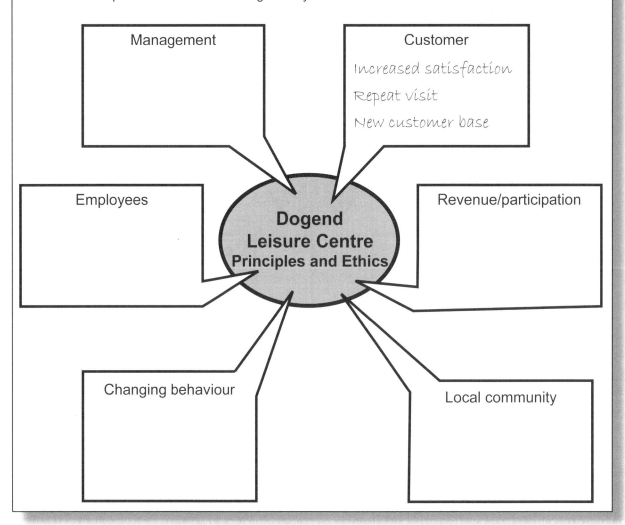

Toolkit: Observing the behaviour of staff towards their customers

This task will involve you visiting a centre and observing the behaviour of staff towards their customers. You can also do this when you are a customer using the facility.

You need to make a judgement on how the centre impacts on its immediate environment. Is there a lot of noise? Is the centre kept in good repair? Is it safe? Is it well lit at night? What impact does that have on the locality?

Finally you need to assess what impact the centre has made on the local community. Does it serve all groups within the community? Does it do this effectively? How does it do this and what could be done to improve this?

Scenario

The management committee of your local leisure facility has commissioned you to complete an ethical audit of their facility and its impact upon the local community. You need to remember that the facility is in the public sector and has a responsibility to serve all sectors of the community. You are to investigate the following:

- The impact that the behaviour of the staff has on its customers.
- The impact of the buildings on the surrounding environment.
- The impact that the Leisure Centre has on the local community.

Having completed this audit, you are to produce a short presentation to give the management committee on your findings, including proposals by which the leisure centre management might improve their performance.

Standards – we all have to have some!

It is generally acknowledged that people in professions have to comply with certain standards. These are normally set by the bodies that regulate these professions. These standards include qualifications, behaviour, confidentiality, professional development, even dress code and apply at national and, often, international, level. For example, lawyers and doctors are expected to keep client confidentiality, teachers are expected to mark pupils fairly, and accountants are expected to produce honest accounts, and so on.

We also have come to expect certain standards of professional sportspersons, but these are not so clearly regulated.

By 2012, coaching will be raised to the level of a profession, recognising its important role in the development of sport and the individuals concerned. Apart from clearly defined ethics and values, coaches will have to meet nationally agreed standards of competence, practice, behaviour and professional development (this means they keep up to date with the latest developments in coaching such as new techniques, research, etc).

Apart from standards that are set by regulating bodies, professionals normally set themselves personal standards relevant to their professional standing. These are standards imposed on themselves – and often expected of their employees, participants or athletes.

For example, the fitness coach of a national athletics squad would not be expected to smoke or drink, or eat unhealthily. Equally, he/she would require his/her athletes to live a healthy lifestyle.

What kind of image do you think it would project if your coach stood by the touchline urging you on, with a cigarette in one hand and a can of lager in the other?

Coaches have to live up to a certain standard because of the expectations generated by their position.

Toolkit: Standards for coaches

Look at the diagram below and try to fill in the blank boxes with the groups of people you think expect standards of the coach.

Groups who expect high standards of a coach

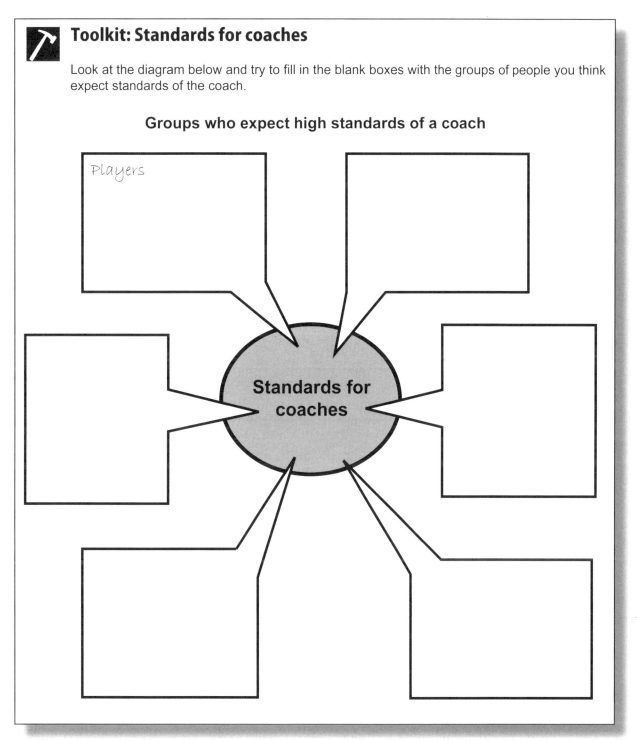

As you have realised by now, standards are important if you want to portray a professional image and lead by example. Meeting professional standards are the hallmark of a true "professional".

Toolkit: Professional standards of coaches or managers

In the table below are listed different areas to which professional standards apply. Look at some well-known coaches or managers, such as Alex Ferguson or Clive Woodward, and try to give examples or explain how they meet the standards in these areas. You may wish to think of occasions when coaches have not lived up to their professional standards.

Area of standards	How coaches meet standards
Image	Example: In control, cool and calm, detached, analytical, positive.
Relationship with players	Example: Confidentiality Example not meeting standards: The reported 'boot' incident between David Beckham and Alex Ferguson*
Relationship with fans/spectators	
Relationship with officials and administrators	
Standing in the community	
Lifestyle	
Appearance	
Health and safety	
Relation with opposition coaches	Example: Alex Ferguson's and Arsene Wenger's public disputes.
Language	
Media	
Fairness and equality	

* Alex Ferguson, Manager of Manchester United was alleged to have kicked a boot in anger at the end of a match. The boot hit and slightly injured star midfielder David Beckham.

Standards don't just apply to coaches; they equally apply to athletes, officials and administrators, and employers in the sports industry; in other words, professionals who are involved with a particular sport and the development of individuals and groups. For example, an international football referee would have to be trained to a standard set by FIFA.

Toolkit: Standards of professionals

Think of standards that may apply to apply to the groups below:

Professional group	Standard
Athletes/participants	
Officials and administrators	Example: Referee/umpires: NGB recognised qualification and experience.
Employers/managers	
PE teachers	

Codes of conduct

All governing bodies of sport and many other sports organisations have developed guidelines for principles, standards and ethical behaviour related to participants, organisers, employers, and professionals involved with individuals or groups.

These are called codes of conduct.

A code of conduct for an umpire or referee could include, for example:

- to be impartial
- to respect all the players
- to ensure the rules are apply
- not to allow the crowd to influence his/her decisions.

Toolkit: Create a code of conduct

As a class group, draw up a code of conduct for a proposed festival of sport. This code should include participants, spectators, organisers and coaches/officials.

Author's advice

You may find the following websites useful in helping you to draw up this code of conduct:

www.brianmac.demon.co.uk/ethics.htm

www.hometown.aol.com/beaker625/indexcodeofconduct.html

www.sportengland.org

www.sportscoachuk.org

www.ilam.co.uk
www.isrm.co.uk

Do not forget to also contact the relevant governing bodies of sport for their codes.

Section 4: How does this work in practice?

LO 4:   Plan an activity using principles, ethics and values appropriate to the selected sports activity

The three previous sections have dealt with many of the reasons why it is important to behave ethically. In this section you will apply these principles, ethics and values in a practical setting.

Planning an activity

This section examines the stages when planning and delivering a session. All effective coaching and organisation of an activity demands that you go through the three stages shown in the diagram below:

PLANNING and
ORGANISING

EFFECTIVE
COACHING

COACHING and
HELPING

EVALUATING and
PROGRESSION

Planning sessions and goals

All effective sessions will need to be planned. If this is not done your participants will quickly notice and become dissatisfied, leading to problems with behaviour and motivation.

 Toolkit: Goal planning

Below is a diagram that identifies the whole planning process and how it can assist you in identifying and planning for long-term goals, medium-term goals and short-term goal. It is important that you understand the differences between them. Complete the following statements:

Long-term goals are   _____

Medium-term goals are   _____

Short-term goals are   _____

If you are coaching over a season, or over a year, it is important to plan sections into schemes of work. It is important to know what you want to achieve over an eight-week period or 16-week period. These can then be reviewed and adjusted for the next period.

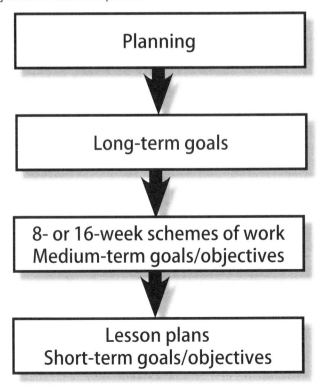

There are a number of important questions you will need to answer when planning your sessions:

- What do the participants want from the sessions?

- What are you trying to achieve during the sessions?

- Do your goals match those of your participants?

- Is it possible to achieve what you want in the time?

- Will the participants find the sessions challenging and rewarding?

- How will you assess whether you have achieved your goals?

- Is this a one-off session or does it build on previous practice?

- What are the main organisational issues that you need to deal with to ensure the session runs smoothly?

Whether you do a one-off session or a number of sessions over a period of time, it is very important to produce individual session plans for your work. There is no one "best way" to produce these, but they should include the following information:

- Organisational issues – the group and their level, numbers in the session, the date, the venue, time, duration of sessions, goals/objectives, equipment required.

- Health and safety issues/reminders – medical conditions/injuries, risk assessment reminder.

- Plan of the session – the structure to include warm-up, main content, cool down and summary, time allocated to each part of the session, organisation and presentation of the session and evaluation.

On the next page is an example of how you might approach structuring your plan.

 Author's advice

In your session plan, you must identify **appropriate principles**, **ethics** and **values**.

Remember, this unit is about ethics and values, not simply about planning a coaching session or how to prepare a session plan.

Therefore, when preparing your evaluation criteria (see the following page) you must relate to principles, ethics and values in your activity.

Toolkit: Designing a session plan

Design your own session plan that incorporates all the information that is identified above and any more that you think is important.

Below is just one example of how you might like to structure your session plan:

SESSION PLAN			
DATE:		VENUE:	
GROUP:		NUMBERS:	
TIME:		DURATION:	
OBJECTIVES:		EQUIPMENT:	
TIME	CONTENT	ORGANISATION	ETHICS/VALUES
RA	MEDICAL CONDITIONS		EVALUATION

How did it go?

The final and arguably most important part of your activity is the evaluation.

Here, you assess your own performance in the session and whether you achieved your objectives or not.

An evaluation requires you to analyse critically – this means you exercise judgement – how you performed and whether or not you met your objectives for the session. You should identify the strengths and weaknesses of your session, and draw conclusions and make recommendations for improvements in future sessions.

It is important that you are honest with yourself because the point of the whole exercise is for you to improve and iron out past mistakes and solve problems.

Why do you think it is so important to go through the process of **evaluation**?

Toolkit: Reasons for evaluating your sessions

With a partner, identify and note reasons why you should evaluate your sessions:

- _____

- _____

- _____

- _____

- _____

- _____

It is important to incorporate **conclusions** and **recommendations**; otherwise you will not improve your coaching sessions. These recommendations should then be reflected in your next session plan.

For example, you are coaching a group of eight- to nine-year-old children in basic ball skills. You have set up some good activities from a coaching book, but the children struggle to follow your instructions and cannot get the activity right. They have trouble with co-coordinating movements and/or hand-eye co-ordination. When you analyse what actually went wrong, you might find the following:

Problem:
Children struggled with your activities and became frustrated.

So, this leads you to the

Conclusion:
Activities too complex and not suitable for the age group.

From this you work out your

Recommendation:
In future sessions, make activities simpler!

Then you have to

Evaluate next session:
Did the activity work better?
If not, make further changes.

As you can see, the whole process of evaluation is a cycle.

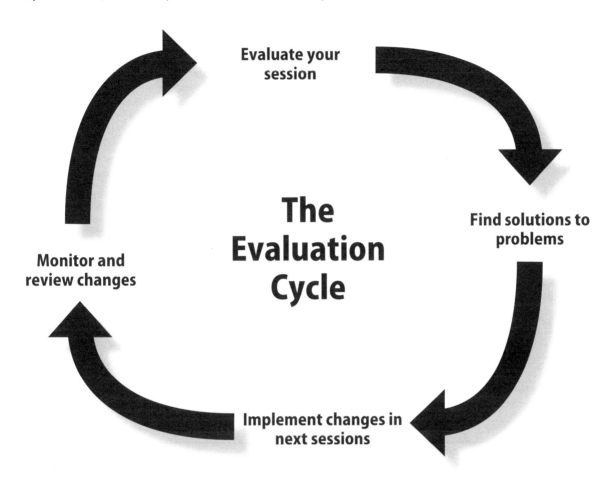

The Evaluation Cycle

Evaluate your session

Find solutions to problems

Implement changes in next sessions

Monitor and review changes

 Author's advice

It is very common for students to write an evaluation that is *descriptive*. In other words, they write about what happened in their session, what they did, what the participants did, etc.

This is **not** the point of an evaluation!

REMEMBER: YOU MUST EVALUATE, NOT DESCRIBE!

How do you find out?

There are the important aspects against which you (or observers) judge your performance.

Examples are:

- safety
- inclusion of all participants
- appropriate language
- suitable activities
- provision for disabled.

These are called **evaluation criteria**.

 ## Toolkit: Prepare evaluation criteria

Look at the key points in your session plan (including ethics and values) and prepare a list of evaluation criteria against which your session can be assessed.

Activities	Evaluation criteria	Yes/No
E.g: Warm-up for the session	• Warm-up structured correctly • Exercises safely done	

Evidence for your assessment

In order to make your evaluation more valid and reliable (it means it is not just solely based on your subjective judgement) it is best to have evidence and feedback supporting your assessment of the session.

There are several ways of getting supporting evidence:

1. You could record your session on video or CD.
2. You can have observation records.
3. You can interview participants and observers.
4. You can hand out feedback/evaluation sheets or questionnaires (see page 173).

1. Recording your session

This is obviously a good way of collecting evidence as the recording is impartial.

The second plus point is that you can view your recorded session. You can see yourself from the position of an observer, which gives you a different perspective of your session. This is a tremendous aid for your session analysis and evaluation.

 Author's advice

It is important if you wish to video the session or interview children to obtain parental/school consent.

2. Observation

If you use observers (these could be your tutor, peers and spectators), you should prepare sheets for them to record their observations. You need these observation sheets as evidence. When designing the observation sheets, make sure you cover the essential points such as your name, the observer's name, location, date, time, aims and content of the session. It is a good idea to include evaluation criteria such as health and safety, a list of all participants, etc.

This then helps you afterwards with your evaluation.

3. Interviews

Remember, you need records as evidence. So you must have a record of your interviews – you can't just say *"I interviewed Mrs Jones and she said I was fantastic."*

So you can either record the interview on tape or CD or make reference to it in your evaluation, or write up a transcript or summary of the interview and ask the interviewee to sign it.

Again, it is a good idea to base your questions on the evaluation criteria so the feedback is geared towards these.

4. Evaluation questionnaires

Questionnaires are not as easily compiled as you might think. They must be compatible with the age group of the participants, e.g. if you coach a group of eight-year-old children, avoid long or complicated words.

Make sure that each question covers only one aspect at a time.

You need to decide what kind of questions you want to ask. There are open-ended questions – these require people to write down their own answers.

E.g.: *What did you think of my session?* _____

This is not a good idea if participants have not got much time or are young children who have trouble writing and formulating their views on paper.

Alternatively, you can ask closed questions where you give people a choice of answers.

E.g.: *In you opinion, was the lesson safely conducted?*   **Yes   No   Not sure**

Sometimes, it is best to ask questions that allow graded or scaled answers.

E.g.: *How do you rate the suitability of the activities?* **Poor   Acceptable   Good   Excellent**

Again, remember to ask questions that give you feedback for your evaluation criteria.

 Author's advice

Make sure you ask the questions in a way that matches the answers.

Example of wrongly posed question

Q. In you opinion, was the lesson safely conducted?

A. Poor   Acceptable   Good   Excellent

You can see, the answer doesn't really match the questions. In this example, the answers provided should be: **Yes   No   Not sure**

Completing the Integrated Vocational Assignment

The culmination of your work for both of the **Sport in Society** and in **Ethics and Values in Sport** units is the completion of your **IVA**, which is a compulsory part of your qualification. If you do not complete this, you may not receive your certificate. Your tutor(s) or lecturer(s) will tell you how long you have to complete the IVA and the access you may have to resources.

Read the IVA carefully and make sure that you understand the work you should hand in and what is required of you. If you are uncertain, discuss it with your tutor(s).

The IVA requires you to work by yourself and to produce original work. You must not share your work with any other learners. If you work in a group at any time, you must present your own responses to each task for assessment.

Evidence can be a mix of written, videoed or taped material. Information taken from sources for research, e.g. Internet and textbooks, must be identified and not presented as your own work. You should list the sources used. Some of the tasks you are to complete may require either observation records or witness statements. You need to check with your tutor(s) that you have these and you must attach them to your submitted work.

IVA completion checklist

Although the content of what you present is most important, you also need to consider the way you present it. You need to make the assessor's task as easy as possible. Remember he/she is marking many assignments, not just yours. Things to consider are:

	✓
Have you completed all the tasks?	
Are all tasks/sub-tasks labelled appropriately?	
Are all pages numbered and your name on each one?	
Are tasks presented in correct order?	
Is all electronic material to be submitted in paper format?	
Have you clearly labelled video or audio tapes that you will submit as part of the assignment?	
Are all of your papers securely bound in a good quality wallet?	

Contents

Unit 4: Health and Safety in Sport

Introduction to the unit

Unit 4: Health and Safety in Sport is a compulsory unit of the National Certificate/Diploma in Sport.

This unit will introduce you to health and safety legislation and the issues you need to be aware of when working in a sports organisation or undertaking sporting activities.

You will have the opportunity to investigate how organisations manage health and safety, and you will be able to recognise ways and means of reducing risks and improving working conditions.

The unit will introduce you to a risk assessment-based approach to health and safety management by teaching you to identify hazards and draw conclusions as to the appropriate risk reduction measures.

Health and Safety in Sport is an internally assessed unit; this means you will have to complete assignment work and provide evidence to meet the grading criteria.

Aims of the unit

Health and Safety in Sport will enable you to identify the important laws and regulations that all sports organisations and providers are required to comply with. You will learn to understand and appreciate their relevance in the working environment in sport.

You will be able to analyse the benefits of good health and safety practices, and learn about techniques of safety management and promotion.

You will be able to comprehend the importance of keeping health and safety records and documentation.

Finally, you will learn how to identify hazards and evaluate risks, and develop appropriate risk control measures.

You can put all the knowledge into practice by investigating the health and safety practices of sports organisations.

What the content will cover

In order to be able to understand the basic principles of health and safety, you will, first, need to learn the key legislation that impacts on sports providers.

This means finding out those Acts of Parliament and regulations that are relevant, and what they require you to do. You will learn where to access information as regards health and safety, and also the roles of the enforcing authorities. At the end of the first section, you should be able to identify key Acts and regulations, and explain their relevance to sports organisations.

Second, you will be introduced to the practice of safety management and techniques of ensuring good health and safety. You will be able to "have a go" at various health and safety documents. With your basic knowledge of legislation, you should be able to design promotional material for selected aspects of health and safety and produce guidelines.

This will allow you to analyse the benefits of good health and safety, and the consequences of bad health and safety in different sports. You will also learn about aspects of security in sport such as crowd control, protection of data, use of CCTV, etc, and you will be able to explain the benefits of health, safety and security.

Third, you will learn about risk assessments. You will have the opportunity to carry out some risk assessments and, by doing so, learn the importance of identifying danger areas and how to eliminate such danger and protect people.

What will I do in class?

Classes will provide you with the necessary knowledge required to complete the assessment activities. Although there will be plenty of opportunities to do some fact finding yourself, the classes will occasionally, particularly for Learning Outcome 1 (legislation), be formal lectures.

However, other areas will give you the opportunity to discuss issues in groups, possibly drawing on your own experience.

If you have access to IT during class time, then you will be able to visit various websites to research or take part in interactive activities such as online risk assessment.

The main aim is to help you understand the importance of health and safety management and your legal responsibilities.

How will I be assessed?

At the end of each section there is one assignment activity relevant to the section's content. These assignment activities are linked to the learning outcomes you are required to meet:

LO1:   **Key legislation and regulations**

LO2:   **Managing and promoting health and safety**

LO3:   **Risk Assessment**

LO4:   **Investigate the benefits of health, safety and security**

The assignment activities are structured in a way that allows you to develop your knowledge to cover the pass criteria as well as higher grades.

 Author's advice

Health and safety can be a bit of a dry subject. Try and relate it to your own experience (you may have a part-time job or are involved in coaching). Think of the consequences if you sustained an injury, or through your own negligence or ignorance, someone else got injured. Treat it like the Highway Code: you must learn it before you can drive on the road safely!

Health and safety – what is it all about?

Over the last 20 years or so, health and safety has become an increasingly important issue in sports. Various incidents, such as the **Hillsborough disaster**, the **Bradford Stadium fire** and the **Lyme Bay tragedy** have led to new legislation and stricter measures. The **Health and Safety Executive** (the health and safety police) has, as a result, taken a tougher stance and is currently considering offences like "**corporate manslaughter**". In other words, an organisation can be found guilty of manslaughter in a court of law.

Working in the field of sports, you need to be aware of the responsibility placed upon you; ignorance is no excuse in the eyes of the law. Not implementing, or the breaking of, health and safety legislation is a criminal offence and can lead to prosecution, fines and, although rarely, imprisonment. For example, the managing director of the company that was responsible for the Lyme Bay tragedy in which four children and a teacher died in coastal waters during a canoeing trip, received a prison sentence although he wasn't even based at the Outward Bound centre.

The general public are prepared to take people to court and are even actively encouraged by law firms, advertising in the media, to sue for any injuries and damages.

As a consequence, insurance companies have become more and more nervous of sports and leisure organisations, and as a result, insurance premiums have risen significantly in the last few years, increasing the financial burden.

Sports and leisure differs substantially from other sectors in so far as facility operators and clubs actively encourage people to participate in inherently hazardous activities. Other sectors, like retail or manufacturing, do not allow members of the public to do something dangerous on their premises.

But how do you stop people from falling over on an ice rink or get hit by a racquet when playing squash? How do you stop children getting fouled, and possibly injured, when playing a competitive game of football or taking part in martial arts?

Some sports are more injury prone than others. For examples, rugby produces the highest number of spinal injuries, football causes a great deal of pressure on the lower limbs, and horse riding accidents can cause paralysis (e.g. "Superman" Christopher Reeves) and fatalities.

Apart from a moral duty to look after people, you also have a legal duty to keep people in your charge or in your facility safe.

Therefore, when working in sports, be it as a facility manager or a coach, professional or volunteer, you need to be aware of health and safety and the responsibility that rests on your shoulders. This is the reason why **Health and Safety in Sport** is a mandatory unit.

Section 1: Learn the rules – then you know how to play

LO 1:   Key legislation and regulations

When you begin a new sport, you have to learn the rules of the sport, the tactics and the skills required. The same goes for health and safety – you must learn the rules (or in this case, the regulations) so you know what you can and cannot do.

The difference is that when you commit a foul in football, you might be sent off, but if you "foul" in health and safety, you might get sent to prison!

Therefore you need to learn and understand some of the key legislation. You don't have to remember all the paragraphs and years, but you must be able to remember:

- that they exist and apply to your situation
- what they require of you.

Apart from the legal obligation, you have the moral duty to protect people in your care or on your premises from any harm. This duty is heightened where children are involved because they do not have the same understanding and awareness of danger.

It is highly unethical to expose children (but also adults) to hazards or let them get involved in activities with a high degree of risk of injury (see **Unit 3: Ethics and Values**).

Toolkit: The most dangerous sports and definitions of health and safety

1. As a little warm-up, find out what are the top ten sports causing injuries and the top five causing deaths. You will find the data in some sports management books or on the **Royal Institute of Public Health** website (**www.riph.org.uk**).

2. Try and find a definition for:

HEALTH: _____

SAFETY: _____

Ignorance is no excuse in the eyes of the law

Working as a coach, teacher or sports centre manager, it is your responsibility to familiarise yourself with the current statutory requirements, including health and safety legislation.

Breach of health and safety is a criminal offence and will be investigated (possibly leading to prosecution) by so-called "enforcing authorities". There are three such authorities: one is the **Health and Safety**

Executive (HSE), which acts as the national health and safety police and has offices in most major towns or cities. Health and safety inspectors have a lot of power; in some respects, more than the police. But their role it is also to give guidance and advice.

The other two enforcing authorities are the local council's **Environmental Health Officers** and **Fire Officers**. These deal with special aspects of health and safety, but have in principle the same roles and powers.

Toolkit: Powers and roles of health and safety inspectors

Find out the powers and roles of health and safety inspectors. A good place to start is the **HSE** website (**www.hse.gov.uk**).

Roles:

- e.g. *guidance and advice* _____

- _____

- _____

- _____

- _____

Powers:

- e.g. *entering premises at any time* _____

- _____

- _____

- _____

- _____

Prosecution in a criminal court can lead to punishment. For breaches of health and safety, this can be in the form of fines and, in rare cases, prison sentences. You can go on the HSE website and find out what these fines and prison sentences are, and also to check on recent prosecution cases.

But that is not all! You might be taken to court under civil law. Civil law covers disputes between two private individuals or parties. If your negligence has caused injury to a person, he or she can sue you in a civil court for damages. This means on top of your fines and/or prison sentence, you may have to pay damages. This can bankrupt you as a person or can cause a small business to collapse.

Toolkit: Role playing a health and safety investigation

In small groups, role play this investigation. One student can play the coach, one the health and safety inspector. The others observe and "judge" afterwards.

Scenario

You are a gymnastics coach. During one of your training sessions, you have failed to secure the asymmetric bars properly (they have been faulty for quite some time; you knew this, but have done nothing about it).

As a result, a young gymnast has suffered a severe injury. The mother has informed the health and safety executive, and you are now facing an investigation.

What is my legal duty?

There are many laws and regulations covering health and safety, and you have to learn some of these. These laws have been passed by **Acts of Parliament**, and are written down. This is called **statute law**, and you can look it up. **Breaches** of statute law are criminal offences for which penalties are imposed.

There is also something called **common law**. This is not written down but is based on historic precedence and case law. Under this law, everyone has a **duty of care**. This means you must not do anything that can cause harm or damage by either your acts or omissions. Common law provides for means of compensation for injury or damage suffered because someone else has neglected his/her duty.

This duty of care applies to health and safety – in other words, you as someone in charge of, say, a group of children or a sports facility have the duty to prevent anybody in your care from coming to harm. If you fail in this duty, you are deemed to be **negligent**.

Toolkit: Examples of negligence

Think of examples that could constitute negligence when taking a group of young children on a sailing trip.

Here's one to start you off:

- <u>Not providing life jackets</u>

- _____

- _____

- _____

- _____

Now try to justify, in two or three sentences, why you think all of the above are breaches of duty of care, i.e. negligence.

What are we talking about?

First though, you have to understand the different terms used. Health and safety texts talk about **Acts**, **Regulations**, **Orders**, **Rules** and **Codes of Practice**.

An Act, as mentioned above, is a piece of legislation passed by parliament. This Act then enables ministers of the crown to pass regulations, which are specific to aspects of health and safety, e.g. noise, under this act. **Orders** and **Rules** give the force of the law to an executive action that activate parts of Acts or regulations.

Codes of Practice (**COP**), or **Approved Codes of Practice** (**ACOP**) are industry guidelines based on best practice. Although they are not compulsory – they are not a law – it is advisable to follow them. You will find that most sports governing bodies or associations have issued a code of practice.

Example: There is no law governing the running of a swimming pool, no regulation to tell you how many lifeguards you have to employ. But most swimming pools will follow the guidelines laid down in the publication, _Safety in Swimming Pools_, which is a **Code of Practice**.

Real case: In 2003, a swimmer drowned in a university pool. The body was found by another swimmer at the bottom of the pool. Only one lifeguard had been on duty at the time. The investigation by the **Health and Safety Executive** concluded that the **Code of Practice (Safety in Swimming Pools)** had not been followed. The code recommends at least two lifeguards at all times. The pool management was prosecuted and fined.

Health and Safety Legislation

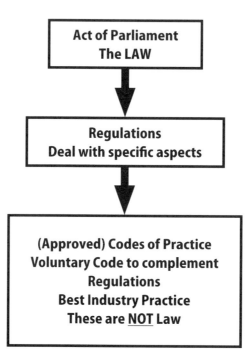

Act of Parliament
The LAW

↓

Regulations
Deal with specific aspects

↓

(Approved) Codes of Practice
Voluntary Code to complement
Regulations
Best Industry Practice
These are <u>NOT</u> Law

 Toolkit: Find more health and safety COPs for sport

1. See if you can find other COPs. You can try sports governing bodies or organisations like the **Institute of Sport and Recreation Management** or the **Fitness Industry Association**.

2. In small groups, now try and develop you own voluntary code for a particular activity or sport.

What do I need to know?

Unless you're a health and safety professional, you can't possibly know every single piece of legislation. But there are some key acts and regulations you must to know.

The most important piece of legislation in the last 30 years is the *Health and Safety at Work Act 1974*.

Health and Safety at Work Act 1974

The *Health and Safety at Work Act* (*HASWA*) introduced for the first time a comprehensive and integrated system for dealing with workplace health and safety and provides a legal framework for promotion of high standards. It consists of four parts. For you as a sports practitioner or manager, only the first part, sections 2–9 (1 is just an introduction) are really relevant. *HASWA* places certain general duties on employers, employees, self-employed and manufacturers and suppliers.

Toolkit: Checking my understanding of legal gobbledygook

Look up the *Health and Safety at Work Act*, either in printed copy or on the Internet. Read sections 2–9 and then briefly summarise the key point of each section. Try to think of an example in a sporting organisation or activity where each key point has relevance (section 5 might be a bit tricky).

Hint: Try the HSE website (**www.hse.gov.uk**).

Section	Key points	Relevance to sport activity/facility
2		
3		
4		
5		
6		
7		
8		
9		

The *Act* requires all employers with five or more employees to have a written health and safety policy.

Find out about it by going on the HSE website and download the sample Health and Safety Policy (this is an excellent document – all you have to do is apply it to your organisation by filling in the blanks).

European health and safety legislation

Another major milestone in the history of health and safety is the *European Directive* or *Framework Directive* (89/391/EEC), in short *FD*. This Directive introduced the so called "**Six Pack**" in 1992, a set of six regulations that have transformed the way health and safety is managed in the workplace (most of the six regulations have been updated since). These regulations are listed in the table below.

Toolkit: Find the key points of the European Directive

Find out the key points and give examples of how they apply to sport facilities or organisations.

Regulation	Key points	Example in sporting/fitness context
Management of Health & Safety at Work Regs.		
Workplace (Health, Safety & Welfare) Regs.		
Provision & Use of Work Equipment Regs.		
Manual Handling Regs.		
Personal Protective Equipment Regs.		
Display Screen Equipment Regs.		

You find all the relevant key legislation and regulations in your unit specification, available from your unit tutor. Information on most of them can be obtained from the **HSE** (**www.hse.gov.uk**) or **Her Majesty's Stationery Office** (**HMSO**) (**www.hmso.gov.uk**) websites.

The HSE also provides a free starter pack for small businesses that includes all necessary key legislation.

Some of the health and safety laws and regulations apply to specific groups and/or areas, for instance the *Children Act 1989* or the *Activity Centre (Young Person's Safety) Act 1996*. The latter was a direct consequence of the Lyme Bay tragedy.

Sports grounds

In recent years, there have been a number of disasters in football stadiums around the world (South Africa, Iran, Ghana). With ever-larger spectator crowds, the safety of football and sports stadiums has become increasingly important.

In the UK, there are two specific Acts that cover safety of sports grounds.

1. *The Safety at Sports Grounds Act 1975*

This *Act* is aimed at stadiums with a capacity of 10,000 spectators or more. It was designed to introduce safety measures to protect spectators. The stadium must meet certain criteria in order to gain the required safety certificate by the local authority. These criteria are:

- a maximum limit of spectators
- separation and grouping of spectators
- certain number of entrances and exits
- seating arrangements
- provision of barriers
- recording of spectator numbers
- keep maintenance records.

Under the *1975 Act*, it was a criminal offence not to have a safety certificate or breaking the requirements.

However, after the fire disaster at the Bradford football ground, the Act was reviewed, and it was found that it was no longer sufficient to deal with the three main problems of **crowd control**, **structural failure** and **fire**.

2. *The Fire Safety, and Safety of Places of Sports Act*

This *Act* was passed in 1987 as a result of the disaster . Unfortunately, it did not prevent the Hillsborough Stadium tragedy in 1989. The ***Taylor Report***, which followed, made more stringent recommendations as regards application of the two Acts and overall safety.

Toolkit: Investigating the *Fire Safety, and Safety of Places of Sports Act 1987* and the *Taylor Report*

1. Find out about the *Fire Safety, and Safety of Places of Sports Act 1987* and the *Taylor Report*. Compare the *1975 Act* with the *1987 Act* and identify the changes and improvement the later *Act* introduced.

2. Identify the recommendations made by the *Taylor Report*.

3. Prepare a short presentation giving your view as to whether the recommendations of the *Taylor Report* could have prevented the Hillsborough disaster. Would a better implementation of the existing legislation in 1987 have been sufficient to prevent the tragedy?

You may have to research the 1989 Hillsborough disaster.

A good website to look at is the **Football Licensing Authority** at **www.flaweb.org.uk**.

You must report injuries! (Well, certain ones)

The **Reporting of Injuries, Diseases and Dangerous Occurrences Regulations 1995** (**RIDDOR**) places the duty on you to report certain injuries to your enforcing authority (either HSE or Local Authority Environmental Health Department). This is to ensure that severe injuries are logged, investigated and analysed so that measures to prevent them recurring in future can be devised (the same applies to diseases and dangerous occurrences).

You don't have to report every injury, only severe ones. These are all listed within **RIDDOR** and include:

*   fractures of major bones (not fingers or toes)
*   dislocation of pelvis, hip, shoulder or knee
*   chemical burns or electrical shocks that lead to unconsciousness
*   any injury that requires resuscitation
*   any injury leading to hospitalisation for more than 24 hours
*   injuries causing blindness (temporary or permanent)
*   any injury leading to an absence from work for more than three days (not counting the day of the injury)
*   asphyxiation and drowning
*   fatalities.

The quickest way to report them is to call the **Incident Contact Centre** (**ICC**) Mondays to Fridays, office hours, on 0845 300 9923. If your need to report outside these hours, you can contact your local HSE office or ring the HSE Info line 08701 545500 or visit the website at **www.riddor.gov.uk**.

If you choose the latter way of reporting, you have to fill in form F2508 and send it to the enforcing authority within ten days (the ICC fill in the form over the phone for you).

Author's advice

You can access and complete the **RIDDOR** form online at **www.hse.gov.uk/forms/**

COSHH – Handle with care!

The Control of Substances Hazardous to Health Regulations 1999 (**COSHH**) state that you must carry out an assessment of any dangerous substances you use (substances can be chemicals, fumes, vapours, dusts and bacteria).

Toolkit: Entry of dangerous substances into the body

There are four ways they can get into your body – what are they?

1. _____

2. _____

3. _____

4. _____

Although the COSHH Regulations apply more to the chemical industry than the sports industry, there are still areas where you have to be aware of hazardous substances. For example, swimming pools use chemicals to disinfect the water and balance its acidity. Commercial drain cleaner contains a high percentage of sulphuric acid that can cause severe chemical burns.

What the regulations ask you to do is assess the danger of substances you use in your organisation. In order to carry out the correct assessment process, you must follow seven steps.

 Toolkit: COSHH assessment steps

1.   List the seven COSHH assessment steps:

i._____

ii. _____

iii. _____

iv. _____

v. _____

vi._____

vii. _____

2.   Once you have found out about these steps, conduct a COSHH assessment for a couple of hazardous chemicals you would expect to find in a sports centre or stadium.

3.   Symbol quiz: All hazardous substances must carry a symbol that identifies its particular danger. Give the symbol that means:

   • irritant

   • flammable

   • toxic

   • corrosive

   • explosive.

 Author's advice

You can find them, and the answer to the question how substances can get into your body in the HSE booklet, *COSHH – a brief guide to the regulations*. It is also available on the HSE website.

Health and Safety at Work (First Aid) Regulations 1981

It is important to remember that accidents can happen any time, anywhere.

The **First Aid Regulations**. require you to meet certain criteria in order to enable first aid to be given to your employees if they are injured or become ill at work. You must provide appropriate equipment, facilities and trained staff.

The minimum requirements are:

* a suitably stocked first-aid box
* an appointed person to take charge of first-aid arrangements.

Your first-aid requirements depend on whether you are classed as a low, medium or high risk work environment. If you are a small organisation with low risk, you only have to make minimum provisions. But if you are rated a higher risk work place (and most sport organisations would), you need to make appropriate provisions such as a First-Aid Room and trained first-aiders.

What should be kept in the first-aid room?

According to the HSE guidance, a first-aid room should contain essential first-aid facilities and equipment. Typical examples of these are:

* a sink with hot and cold running water
* drinking water and disposable cups
* soap and paper towels
* a store for first aid materials
* foot-operated refuse containers, lined with disposable yellow clinical waste bags or a container for the safe disposal of clinical waste
* a couch with waterproof protection, clean pillows and blankets
* a chair
* a telephone or other communication equipment
* a record book for recording incidents where first aid has been given.

Toolkit: Spot the deliberate mistakes

Which of the contents of a first-aid box listed below should not be in it?

Put a tick against the items that SHOULD be included in the first-aid box and a cross against those that should not.

	✓/X
20 individually wrapped, sterile, adhesive dressings of assorted sizes.	
Two sterile eye pads.	
One packet of aspirins.	
Four individually wrapped triangular bandages (preferably sterile).	
Six safety pins.	
One tube of cream for burns.	
Six medium-sized (approximately 12 cm x 12 cm) individually wrapped, sterile, unmedicated wound dressings.	
Two large (approximately 18 cm x 18 cm) sterile, individually wrapped, unmedicated wound dressings.	
One can of anti-inflammatory spray for insect bites.	
One pair of disposable gloves.	
Three disposable syringes.	

Author's advice

If you are not sure, you can look the correct content up in the HSE leaflet, *Basic advice on first aid at work* or on **www.hse.gov.uk/pbuns/firindex.htm**, *First Aid at Work: Your questions answered*.

Hot stuff – Fire!

Statistically, you will come across a fire situation twice in you lifetime. One in four people will encounter a life threatening fire in his/her lifetime. Fires cost hundreds of lives every year and destroys millions of pounds worth of property.

Some fires have disastrous proportions; just think of the Bradford Stadium fire, or the fire that burnt down a Center Parcs resort in Thetford.

Fire is associated with a number of potentially fatal hazards:

* burns
* smoke
* toxic fumes
* structural collapse.

The fire triangle

In order to exist, fire needs three things:

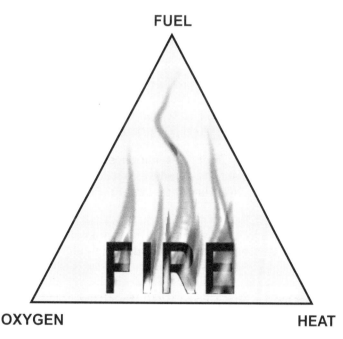

FUEL

OXYGEN   **HEAT**

If you take one of these components away, the fire will die. That's exactly what fire extinguishers do. For instance, water cools = no heat!

In order to prevent a fire starting, you must eliminate or reduce the risk of the fire triangle coming together. For example, it would not be clever to store chemicals or paper next to a hot boiler.

A lot of fires are caused by cigarettes; often, cigarette stubs are thrown on with general rubbish at the end of a shift in a pub or bar. If they have not been properly extinguished, they can re-ignite and start a fire.

Toolkit: Fire prevention

List some basic measure you could introduce to reduce fire risk:

- e.g. *No smoking signs* _____
- _____
- _____
- _____
- _____

Fire legislation

Approach to fire safety has changed over the past years. A lot of earlier legislation and regulations have been amended and updated. Generally, a more risk management-based approach has taken over from prescriptive rules and regulations.

The major act here is the ***Fire Precautions Act 1971***, which introduced Fire Certificates for premises, and the **Fire Precautions (Workplace) Regulations 1997**, which required **Fire Risk Assessments**.

The new Regulatory Reform (Fire Safety) Order 2004 introduces a new, risk-based approach to fire safety and revokes the *Fire Precautions Act*. This means, from 2005, Fire Certificates will be abolished. Instead, all employers must carry out a **Fire Risk Assessment** (**FRA**). **Proformas** for **FRAs** can be obtained from the Fire Officer.

You have to **manage** fire safety. This means you have to have **fire warning systems**, **sufficient** and **appropriate fire fighting equipment**, **emergency procedures**, **system maintenance logs** and **training records**.

Toolkit: Fire training for a football stadium

What kind of fire training do you think staff in a large football stadium should have?

Toolkit: Fire quiz – know your extinguishers

Find out what type of fire extinguishers exist, what they contain and on what type of fire you can use them!

Extinguisher band colour	Extinguisher content	Use on what type of fire
Red		
Beige		
Black		
Blue		
Fire blanket		

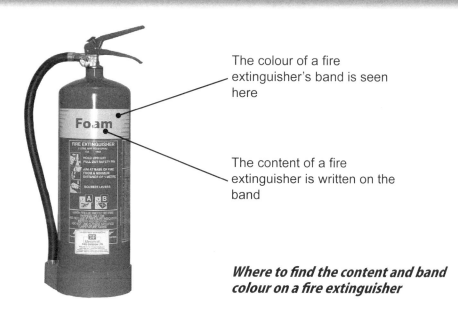

The colour of a fire extinguisher's band is seen here

The content of a fire extinguisher is written on the band

Where to find the content and band colour on a fire extinguisher

Toolkit: Carry out a fire risk assessment

1. Obtain a **FRA** form (printed copy or soft copy) and carry out a fire risk assessment for your organisation's sports areas. Compare this with a more vulnerable area such as a chemistry laboratory. Identify the differences and high risk areas.

2. Investigate the fire prevention systems and fire emergency procedures at the organisation. For example, what fire warning system is being used, what type of fire fighting equipment is in place, what is the evacuation procedure?

3. Check out the fire signs and fire exits. Are the signs appropriate? Are the exits and fire doors properly marked and kept clear?

 Tutor talk

Your tutor might be able to arrange for someone in your school/college to show you and explain the fire warning system.

Most fire services have an education department or officer. It might be worthwhile contacting them to arrange a visit.

Disability discrimination

In October 2004, the last part of the *Disability Discrimination Act 1995* (**DDA**) came into force. The *DDA* makes it illegal to discriminate against disabled people on grounds of their disability. Sports organisations as providers of services and facilities are very much affected by the *DDA*.

 Toolkit: Investigating the *Disability Discrimination Act 1995*

1. Look up the *DDA* on the Internet. You may want to go on the **Disability Rights Commission** website (**www.drc.gov.uk**) to find out about the *Act*, its implications and prosecution cases.

2. You are a sports centre manager. Write a short memo to your staff outlining the main requirements of the *DDA* and its impact on the centre.

Don't work your staff into the ground! – the *European Working Time Directive*

This *Directive* sets out rules as to how long staff should work, what the rest time between shifts should be and what breaks employees are entitled to. For example, employees must have at least 11 hours rest between the end of one shift and the beginning of the next. This affects leisure centres with long opening hours.

Toolkit: Give me a break!

Look up the *Working Time Directive* and list the main points below The **Department for Trade and Industry** (**DTI**) has published a leaflet with the main points of the legislation. You can get this online on at **www.dti.gov.uk**.

- _____

- _____

- _____

- _____

- _____

- _____

Personal data – keep it a secret!

In 1984, the *Data Protection Act* was first introduced. It had a major impact on the handling, storing and access to personal data. It gave individuals certain rights regarding personal information held by others such as the council, companies and medical records.

Under the *Act*, you have the right to see all information held about you by, say, your employer or your local authority. Also, all personnel records, like your personal file, must be kept safe and secure and not be accessible to someone else.

As a result of this *Act*, the official accident book was changed at the beginning of 2004 because it allowed other people to look up personal information such as addresses and date of birth as recorded in the accident book. Now, pages are perforated so they can be torn out and kept in a secure place.

 Toolkit: Find out about your rights!

1. Look up the *Data Protection Act* (on the web or a printed copy) and familiarise yourself with the main points of the *Act*.

2. Describe the relevance of the *Act* for a sports organisation

Child protection

Unfortunately, sports organisations can sometimes be places of child abuse. Young children are very vulnerable and can be exposed to abuse if the organisations in whose care they are do not take their duties seriously.

The law recognised this fact two decades ago when it passed the *Children Act* in 1984. This *Act* gives a child basic rights, but also places responsibilities on those who have access to or work with children, e.g. coaches and youth leaders. One major requirement is that all those who work with children must have police clearance. This is called a **CRB check** – **CRB** stands for **Criminal Records Bureau**.

 Toolkit: Investigating the *Children Act*

1. Find out your responsibilities under the *Children Act* – you can look up the *Act* on the web.
2. Read the following scenario and complete the task that follows it:

Scenario

You have just been employed as the new head coach for a swimming club. After the first few weeks you notice that Fred, an assistant volunteer coach who has been with the club for over 20 years, is making a lot of physical contact with the children when explaining things. For example, he is holding their arms when demonstrating strokes, and supports them on the starting blocks when teaching shallow dives. He also often pats the children's backs for encouragement. After the training session, you see him going into the boys' changing room to talk to the children about the next competition.

As part of your coach education, you have been on child protection courses. You know that Fred is only trying to be friendly, but you also realise that his conduct leaves him and the club wide open for possible allegations. You decide to call Fred into your office and talk to him.

Task

How would you address your concerns with Fred? You expect Fred to react adversely and defensively, so you have to present your arguments in a convincing manner.

Role play

This scenario presents an opportunity for role play. Two students can act as the coach and Fred.

Despite child protection legislation, cases of abuse have come to light in recent years. As a result, the **NSPCC** and **Sport England** got together and formed the **Child Protection in Sport Unit** (**CPSU**) in 2001.

The role of the CPSU is to give help and guidance with child protection. All sports organisations that receive public sector or Sport England funding are required to have a child protection policy.

As part of coach education, a coach is required to complete a sports specific or generic child protection workshop.

Guidance, advice and counselling are available from the **NSPCC** (**www.nspcc.org.uk**), phone 0808 800 5000 and **ChildLine** (**www.childline.org.uk**), phone 0800 1111.

Toolkit: Child protection policy

1. Identify four forms of child abuse (the CPSU website **www.cpsu.co.uk** might give you some help):

   * _____

   * _____

   * _____

   * _____

2. Try and develop a child protection policy for a chosen sport.

3. Compare you policy with the one of the national governing bodies of that sport and the sample policy on the CPSU website.

Identify key legislation

 Toolkit: Mix and match key legislation

Identify the key legislation and regulations, and their relevance for sporting organisations/facilities.

In the table below are listed the general areas of health and safety you have to be cover in a sports centre. Identify the legislation, regulations and requirements you have to meet within each area and list the requirements.

A list of the applicable regulations is at the end of this section, but DON'T look until you've tried it yourself!

Area	Act/Regulation	Requirements
Health and safety policy	Health and Safety at Work Act	Written policy incl. statement, arrangement and organisation
General safety arrangements		
Accident arrangements		
Fire safety		
Food preparation		
Training		
Handling chemicals		
Electrical equipment		
Accident reporting		
Use of computers		
Moving heavy loads		
Safe use of equipment (incl. sunbeds)		

Toolkit: Mix and match key legislation (continued)

Area	Act/Regulation	Requirements
Welfare facilities		
Children's activities		
Disabled facilities		
Premises are safe for visitors		
Personal records		
Staff working hours		
Goggles and gloves		

By now you should be very confident in identifying the main pieces of legislation that are relevant to sports organisations and facilities. You should be able to find sources of information such as the HSE, Sport England and National Governing Bodies of Sport.

So are you ready to face your first assessment activity?

Assessment activity 1: Get your first tick in the box!

LO 1   Key legislation and regulations

Dodgy FC

Scenario

You have been offered the job of operations manager of 'Dodgy Football Club' (Nickname: The 'Bodgers'). The club plays in the First Division and has an older, 30,000 seater stadium. It has been struggling financially for a while and has, as a result, cut quite a few corners. Before you accept the job, you have decided to check the things out "incognito" during the next match.

To your absolute horror, you find the following during your undercover inspection:

- There are not enough stewards on duty, most of them watch the match and not the crowds.
- Banks of broken chairs have been taken out and not replaced; spectators are permitted to stand in the space.
- The ground has broken glass and even dogs' faeces on it.
- The match is against a top team and has attracted lots of spectators. You're convinced that more than 30,000 people have been admitted in order to take as much gate money as possible.
- Some of the emergency signs are broken and have partly been replaced by "home-made signs" in various colours.
- Cables run across aisles to the burger stand.
- The cook in the burger stand uses the same kitchen implements for raw and cooked meat.
- The rubbish bins have not been emptied after the last match.
- Along the corridor to the restaurant, a cleaner is mopping the floor; there is no "caution – wet floor" sign.
- In the bar, you noticed some youngster being served alcohol.
- The first-aid boxes contain creams and aspirins, and there appears to be no accident book on site.
- In the plant room, you trip over loads of old cardboard boxes and pieces of timber.
- Outside two fire exits, contractors have stored their building materials.
- Cleaning chemicals are stored outside the changing rooms and are kept in unmarked containers.
- You've noticed an older odd-job man struggling to shift some heavy equipment by himself.
- There seems to be no information as to health and safety, no emergency contacts or numbers, no posters.
- The health and safety policy consists of a two-page document listing evacuation procedures. The policy was last reviewed in 1995.
- The electrical equipment has no "pass" stickers on it.
- You spotted several wires that have been fixed with tape.
- There is no risk assessment and no fire risk assessment.
- Several fire detection devices are missing. You're told they're in the maintenance office for repair. There is no test log.
- There seems to be no maintenance log, and quite a few of the tools still carry the B.S. kite mark.
- There is a dedicated area for wheelchair users, but when fans stand up the wheelchair users can't see. They can't get to the first floor bar and have to send someone up to take their order.
- When checking the personnel files, you realise that two coaches helping with youth training have not been CRB checked. There is no child protection policy in place for youth coaching.

Prepare a report for the board of the club identifying the key legislation and regulations that Dodgy FC is breaching. Explain the impact of the legislation and the potential consequences for the club, and make recommendations as to what action needs to be taken.

List of regulations for Toolkit (Mix and Match) (Note that this list is not in any particular order):

- Management Regulations
- Electricity at Work Regulations
- Display Screen Equipment Regulations
- Provision and Use of Work Equipment Regulations
- Manual Handling Regulations
- *Health and Safety at Work Act*
- European Working Time Directive
- *Data Protection Act*
- *Disability Discrimination Act*
- *Children Act*
- Workplace Regulations
- Reporting of Injuries, Diseases and Dangerous Occurrences Regulations
- Control of Substances Hazardous to Health Regulations
- *Food Safety Act*
- *Occupier's Liability Act.*

Section 2: Health and safety is no good if no one knows about it!

L02:   Investigate how an organisation manages and promotes health and safety

One problem that often occurs with health and safety is that it is not communicated to all employees or others that may be involved in a sports organisation/event. Having a folder with all the required documentation sitting in the bottom drawer of your desk is no good; all people involved in running a sports organisation, particularly the ones who conduct and supervise activities, need to know the relevant standards and requirements. This applies to sports and leisure centres, private fitness clubs, Outward Bound centres and voluntary clubs alike.

As mentioned in *Section 1*, since the European "Six Pack", a management approach to health and safety has been introduced; in other words, the law requires organisations to manage health and safety. This means recognising that health and safety has to be regularly monitored and reviewed, new measures have to implemented, new rules and policies be communicated, staff be trained, and that the support of all involved has to be gained.

Procedures

Managers of organisations have to put policies in place (such as a health and safety policy, which is required under the HASWA), and devise and implement certain health and safety procedures.

The two main procedures any organisation should have are:

1. **Normal Operating Procedure (NOP)**

2. **Emergency Action Plan (EAP)**

NOP: Most larger sports organisation, in particular those who run facilities, will have NOPs. These outline the day-to-day running of the organisation and include information on opening hours, operating areas, setting up of equipment, staff clothing, where equipment is stored, reporting structures, fire alarm testing, water testing, training, first aid, accident reporting, cashing-up procedures, etc.

The purpose of the NOP is to set out clearly all that is required to run an organisation such as a sports centre smoothly. Anyone unsure, or new employees, can look it up, and it should form part of the induction of new employees.

EAP: The purpose of an EAP is to tell you what to do if things don't run smoothly and an emergency has occurred. It will detail things like fire and evacuation procedures, what to do in case of an accident, power failure, structural problems, emission or spillage of toxic substances, bomb alarm and other emergencies. It will also allocate roles and responsibilities to certain persons. For instance:

> *"In case of fire, the gym instructors evacuate the fitness gym, the lifeguards the swimming pool!"*

It is important that all members of staff and/or volunteers, coaches, etc, know the EAP because they must react in the correct way in the event of an emergency. Therefore, the EAP should be a regular part of staff training and must be part of the induction.

Toolkit: Design a sports centre

You are to design a sports centre (don't go too mad). In your plan, mark emergency exits and evacuation routes, first-aid room and positions for first-aid boxes, fire alarm panel and fire assembly point.

Then draw up in bullet point format:

1. an NOP

2. an EAP.

In addition to your NOP and EAP, you must devise and implement safe systems of work. These are safety procedures for more hazardous jobs such as working with electricity, in confined or high space, or lone work. For example, if you were working with electricity, you wouldn't want someone else to switch the power back on whilst you're holding bare wires in your hand. Therefore, you must think of ways to prevent this happening, i.e. a safe system of work.

Accidents

What actually is an accident?

An accident is defined as an unplanned event leading to injury, damage or loss.

Who or what causes accidents?

Health and safety literature recognises three major factors that lead to accident and injuries:

1. **Occupational factors** – these are inherent in the nature of the job, e.g. a professional boxer runs a high risk of getting injured.

2. **Environmental factors** – these are caused by the working environment, e.g. heat, cold, noise, radiation.

3. **Human factors** – accidents caused by human failure. This is usually the main factor. Fatigue, lack of training, ignorance, apathy, etc, can all lead to accident and injury.

Real case: In a public swimming pool, lifeguards were messing around in the water after the end of their shift. Some of them were diving into the shallow end despite this being against the rules. The lifeguards knew they were breaking these safety rules. One of them struck the floor and broke his neck, and became paralysed as a result. The case went to court and both the pool operator and the lifeguard were found to be negligent.

Author's advice

If somebody is not following your health and safety instruction or company policy, then you have to reprimand and even discipline that person. If you don't, then you can be seen as condoning bad practice, and in the event of an accident, you can be partly negligent (this is called contributory negligence).

Toolkit: Examples of occupational, environmental and human factors

Using the table below, list examples for each factor and then state what you could do to about it.

Factors	Sporting example	Corrective action
Occupational factor		
Environmental factor		
Human factor		

Carry out regular checks!

Ensure that your safety procedures are working and your systems are functioning. This is called an audit. You also need to ensure that your premises and equipment are safe and secure. This is called an inspection.

The best way of carrying out an inspection is to design a checklist covering all areas and safety criteria/standards.

For example:

Area	Item	Achieved Yes/No	Action
Sports hall	Floor even, no trip hazards	Y	None required
	Floor clean and non-slip	N	Clean floor, review cleaning schedule, remind attendants

At the end of the inspection, you can evaluate the results by expressing the achieved items in percentage terms, e.g. 85% means that out of all items inspected, 85% were ticked "Yes" in the Achieved box.

Toolkit: Produce an inspection check list

Produce an inspection checklist for a facility you have access to and carry out an inspection. Analyse the findings and propose measures for improvement.

Prevention is better than cure

The whole purpose of managing and promoting health and safety is accident prevention.

You have already learned a bit about the benefits of accident prevention, and the possible consequences of not doing so.

The **Institution of Occupational Safety and Health** (**IOSH**) recognises three key objectives of accident prevention:

1. **Moral**: You have a moral obligation towards people in your care and must protect them from harm so far as reasonably possible. Remember your **Duty of Care**!

2. **Legal**: Because the law says so, and you will be prosecuted and punished if you don't comply.

3. **Economic**: Paying out for legal bills, damages and fines can be costly for a business.

We will come back to these objectives later on in *Section 4*.

In order to understand accidents (remember: unplanned events leading to harm, damage or loss) you need to understand what causes accidents. As mentioned before, the biggest cause is the **human factor**.

Toolkit: A chain reaction!

Studies show that most accidents are not caused by one single factor but by a chain of events that eventually culminate in the accident. Read the following case study:

Case study

The lat pull-down machine in a fitness gym has not been maintained for a while because there is a shortage of instructors and the gym is very busy. One of the cables has started to fray. It has been noted by staff and customers, but no one has officially reported it, and it has not been put in the maintenance log book.

It is now so bad that a customer complains to the supervisor. He promises to repair it straight away, but then has to take a long phone call. He forgets to tell another instructor. A new gym-user, who hasn't had an induction owing to the instructor shortage, comes along and tries to test his strength at the lat pull-down machine. He stacks up a lot of weights and then pulls down with all his strength. The frayed cable finally snaps and the customer smashes the steel handlebar on his neck vertebrae, fracturing it.

Draw the events described in the case study in a time line and then decide at which point along the chain the accident could have been prevented.

Get everybody behind you!

One of the major challenges any organisation faces is creating a "health and safety culture". This is only possible if people are informed and trained. As you know by now, information and training is a duty imposed on employers under the *Health and Safety at Work Act*. The *Act* also makes it an absolute duty to have a written **health and safety policy** in which the employer must set out a statement of health and safety, arrangements and organisation.

How these requirements translate into practice is that you must display the **Health and Safety Law poster** in the workplace, keep employees up to date on health and safety issues, consult with them on a regular basis (where trade unions are involved, a health and safety representative must be appointed by law, but it might be a good idea to have a health and safety officer anyway). Safety officers must be allowed time off for training and to deal with health and safety issues.

Most importantly, you must hold regular staff training sessions (adequate training is a requirement under the Management of Health and Safety at Work Regulations 1999).

A record of these sessions (what the topic was, who attended) should be kept. Some of the training will be general, such as fire evacuation, some will be very specific, for instance first-aid training or chemical handling for plant-room operators in swimming pools. Other training sessions might be about special equipment or tools (can you remember which regulation stipulates training for equipment?).

 Toolkit: Developing a health and safety training programme

Develop a health and safety training programme for attendants in a leisure centre. Think carefully about the issues you need to cover.

Example health and safety training program

Training topic	Specifics	When/how often	Who	Training provider	Comments
Fire	Evacuation	Six monthly	All staff and instructors	Internal	Compulsory attendance
	Extinguisher training	Annually	All staff	Fire brigade	Compulsory attendance Personal certificate

Reporting and documentation

The importance of reporting and recording faults, accidents and injuries must not be underestimated (that's why there is a specific regulation – can you name it?).

The reason for reporting is to draw awareness to a fault, problem or injury/accident. You cannot deal with, say, a faulty and dangerous piece of gym equipment if nobody tells you about it. Once it has been reported, you must deal with it, otherwise you would be grossly negligent and wouldn't even have the excuse that you didn't know about the problem.

Keeping records will also help safeguard your position in case of claims. Unfortunately, in the current, so-called "litigation culture", organisations must play the "paperwork game". Claimant solicitors have developed a tactic of demanding to see a long list of your health and safety paperwork.

Therefore, the purpose of recording is twofold:

1. To analyse and investigate the incident. If you decide to investigate the accident, record your findings.
2. To protect yourself from possible litigation. If you have documented the facts and have taken witnesses' names and addresses, then these facts cannot later on be disputed by a third party.

Author's advice

Under current legislation, people have three years to submit a claim for personal injury. So you must keep your records such as accident book, risk assessment, training records, etc, for several years.

Toolkit: Design an accident report form

Design an accident report form. What type of information is essential? What is desirable?

Warning

In case of an injury, never give medical advice!
Only a qualified medical professional can do this. It can be held against you!

Accident analysis

One reason for recording accidents is so you can analyse them on a regular basis. This will enable you to identify problem areas and take corrective action.

If you discovered that a particular type of accident occurs quite often in the same spot, then this would indicate a health and safety problem such as hazardous equipment or environment, or lack of supervision. An investigation is then required.

For example, your accident book records a lot of head injuries (cuts and bruises) on one of the giant waterslides in your leisure pool. They all seem to occur at the last bend. This could mean the bend is too sharp and throws riders about, causing them to bang their head against the side of the slide. Having identified this as the cause, you must take steps to eliminate it. If you don't, you're negligent.

The best way of analysing accidents is to categorise them using criteria such as type of injury (fracture, concussion, cuts, bruises, etc), part of the body, location within facility (gym, pool, changing room), type of activity (football, squash), and causes (slip, bad tackle, faulty equipment). Setting up a spreadsheet with all those criteria is an effective way of analysing accidents and injuries.

Accident analysis is good practice and demonstrates you are a responsible operator/organisation that takes their duty of care seriously.

 Toolkit: Accident analysis

Using a spreadsheet, set up an accident analysis form for an indoor ski centre.

Accident investigation

 Toolkit: Investigate a serious accident

The report should be impersonal and factual, stating what happened, information gathered during the investigation, and details of witnesses. It should finish with conclusions and recommendations.

Scenario

Let's assume the worst – a serious accident has happened during an under 10s' holiday activity; a child was badly injured and had to be taken to hospital in an ambulance.

The accident has been duly reported and recorded; you, as the manager, must now investigate the incident.

There are several reasons for this:

1. Enforcement agencies will look for evidence of blame.

2. Claim specialists will look for evidence of liability.

3. You, as the organiser, need to establish whether a reoccurrence can be prevented.

There should be a defined procedure in place; forms and checklists will help concentrate attention on the important details. Once the investigation is concluded, a report should be written that should give answers to the questions:

*   What were the immediate causes of the accident?

*   Were there any other causes that contributed to it?

*   What necessary corrective action is required?

*   What changes are needed to prevent reoccurrence?

*   What policy and/or procedural changes are required?

The above accident during an under 10s' holiday activity happened to a nine-year-old boy who, while sitting out during a basketball match, had slipped away with a friend and decided to scale the 9m high climbing wall at the end of the sports hall. Half way up the wall, he lost his grip and fell to the sports hall floor. His friend alerted the activity supervisor, who found the boy unconscious. One leg was at an awkward angle, indicating a bad fracture. The boy regained consciousness, but had to be taken to hospital by ambulance.

In small groups, acting the roles of friend, activity supervisor and investigator, carry out an accident investigation. Using the form on the following page, write a short report following the above guidance, giving conclusions and recommendations.

State if any changes in policies and/or procedures will be necessary to prevent a similar accident in the future. State whether, in your view, the accident was foreseeable and, as such, preventable.

Don't elaborate too much when apportioning blame. Pointing the finger is not the right way forward in establishing a health and safety culture in an organisation; constructive criticism, education and collective responsibility is.

ACCIDENT INVESTIGATION FORM

DATE:	TIME:

INVESTIGATOR:

NATURE OF ACCIDENT:

NAME OF INJURED PARTY:	
DATE OF BIRTH:	
ADDRESS:	
TELEPHONE No:	
REPORTABLE UNDER RIDDOR?	HSE INFORMED: YES NO
SUPPORTIVE MATERIAL ATTACHED (DIAGRAMS, PHOTOS, etc.)	SPECIFY:

WITNESSES:
1:
2:

DETAILS OF ACCIDENT: (NOTE: THIS SECTION OF THE FORM WOULD NORMALLY BE LARGER)

CONCLUSIONS/RECOMMENDATIONS (NOTE: THIS SECTION OF THE FORM WOULD NORMALLY BE LARGER)

SIGNATURE OF INVESTIGATOR:

Be positive!

Studies have shown that positive messages are far more successful than negative ones (or warnings) because people usually take the view that "it's not going to happen to me". Health and safety propaganda really should aim to reinforce better quality of work and the work environment, and customer satisfaction.

One good way of making staff more alert to safety issues is carrying out a hazard spotting exercise. Also, encourage your staff to report anything broken, faulty or out of the ordinary instead of leaving it until somebody notices it.

Make it clear to your staff that you, as their employer, need their co-operation in order to provide a safe working environment. Ensure that health and safety management is accepted by everyone and that it applies to all areas and activities of the organisation.

To summarise

The key elements of health and safety management and promotion are:

- To gain support from all people involved in the organisation.
- To motivate, train and educate to raise awareness of health and safety.
- To inspect, audit and consult to obtain feedback.
- To ensure supervisors enforce health and safety.
- To design workable policies and control measures.
- To maintain records and documentation.
- To control hazards and risks.
- To continually review.
- To comply with the current law.

 Toolkit: In your defence

The report should be impersonal and factual, stating what happened, information gathered during the investigation, and details of witnesses. It should finish with conclusions and recommendations.

Scenario

You are the general manager of a large leisure pool. One day you receive a letter from somebody claiming that he sustained a cut on your waterslide. That cut, the letter further claims, became infected by bacteria in the pool water.

The author of the letter makes the allegation that your slide is poorly maintained and that the quality of the pool water is extremely poor. He is threatening to take legal action against you for negligence.

What documents/records could you check and use in your defence to refute that allegation?

Discussion point: Your assistant manager suggests offering the person some money as compensation. Do you think this is a good idea? What is the potential problem with offering financial compensation?

Assessment activity 2: Produce promotional material

LO2:   Managing and promoting health and safety

The Dodgy FC board is so impressed with your report that they have asked you to produce a guidance leaflet for health and safety. This, of course, is a big task; therefore, you have to prioritise where to start first. You decide to address the most urgent health and safety issue first.

1.   From among the list of problems identified on page 204, choose the one that in your view needs tackling first. Explain why you have chosen this particular issue as priority and then produce promotional material (guidance notes, poster, etc) for your target audience.

2.   Explain the promotional material (i.e. the reason why you chose a particular type, distribution method, etc).

3.   Critically analyse the use of your promotional material, making suitable changes and recommendations. In other words, examine how well the material works in terms of reaching the target audience and eliminating the hazard or reducing the risk.

Section 3: Reduce the risks!

LO3:   Produce risk assessments for a variety of hazards

All the latest changes in health and safety legislation support a much more management-based approach. The most crucial piece of legislation is the **Management of Health and Safety at Work Regulations 1992** (reviewed in 1999).

These Regulations require every employer with five or more employees to carry out a written risk assessment. This means you must check out all the workplace hazards and anything else that could potentially harm anybody during an activity.

For example, if you plan a sports day on a hot July afternoon with a large number of younger children, you must anticipate anything that might cause injury or harm to them.

 Author's advice

Bear in mind that when parents leave their children in your care, you are what is called **in loco parentis**; it means "in place of the parents". In other words, you're totally responsible for them. If anything happens to them, or they do something stupid, you could be in trouble.

What actually is a HAZARD and RISK?

Before we go any further, we need (yet again) to clarify a few key words we will be using (and have used, for that matter).

What is a HAZARD?   **Answer:** Anything that has the potential to cause harm.

Examples:

Water in a swimming pool, free weights in a gym, sticks in hockey.

What is RISK?   **Answer:** The likelihood that the hazard will cause harm.

Examples:

How likely is it that a person will drown in the water, hurt himself/herself with the free weights, get hit in the face by the stick?

It is easy to confuse **hazard** and **risk**; just remember **hazard** describes the potential to cause harm, **risk** is the chance of it happening.

What do I have to do and where do I start?

The Management Regulations expect you to identify all the things that are potentially dangerous (**hazards**) and assess how likely it is that anything happens (**risk**). You then must check that what you're already doing will be sufficient to prevent accidents. If not, then you are required to make sure, as far as **reasonably possible**, that either the hazard is taken out or reduced or, if that is not possible, the risk minimised.

In other words, you must **manage** health and safety.

You find the word **reasonable** frequently used in health and safety legislation. It means what can be reasonably expected when balancing the cost of taking safety measures against the risk being considered. The law asks: "What would a reasonable person do?"

How do I carry out a risk assessment?

The HSE booklet, *Five Steps to Risk Assessment*, sets out the basic process of how to carry out a risk assessment. The booklet recommends not overcomplicating the risk assessment because in many working environments, the hazards are few and simple. You're really only supposed to record the **significant** findings of your assessment. You can download the booklet for free from the HSE website (**www.hse.gov.uk**).

However, sometimes, a more detailed risk assessment may be necessary, particularly if a highly hazardous environment or high risk groups are involved (e.g. children on an abseiling course).

The basic recommended steps are:

STEP 1:   **Identify the hazards**. Ignore trivial things and concentrate on the **significant hazards** that could lead to serious injury.

STEP 2:   **Consider who might be harmed**, and in what way. Don't just think of your own staff or the group you're in charge of; there might be others such as cleaners, contractors, visitors, members of the public, etc. Young people, trainees and pregnant women are at particular risk.

STEP 3:   **Evaluate the risk**. The best way of doing this is by grading it, for instance HIGH, MEDIUM, LOW or on a scale of 1–5. How you do it is up to you.

You must then decide whether your existing measures are sufficient or whether more needs to be done. This is really the crucial part of the risk assessment because you have to look very carefully at what you're doing. You should ask yourself whether there are any legal requirements you must meet, and whether you are complying with codes of practice or guidelines. You're aim is it to make all risks non-existent or small.

If you find more action needs to be taken, draw up an action list in order of priority (that's why you graded the risks; the HIGH ones need tackling first).

STEP 4:   **Record your findings** (only if you have five or more employees).

You must write down the **significant hazards** and conclusions (the best way to do this is to carry out the whole risk assessment in a table format; see example). This is important because you must be able to prove that you carried out a suitable and sufficient risk assessment.

STEP 5:   **Monitor**, **review** and, when necessary **revise** your risk assessment.

This means checking frequently that your control measures are really working. Sometimes, the circumstances change, or you introduce new equipment or activities, so you must make sure that your risk assessment is still relevant, or whether it is necessary to introduce new or better measures.

For example, you have a risk assessment for children's summer camp activities. But this year, you introduce trampolining. This is a dangerous activity which, if not carefully supervised, can easily lead to injuries. Therefore, you should check your risk assessment and update it to include trampolining. Revised control measures could mean a better supervisor/children ratio, clear set-up, Instructions, etc. These five steps are a simple way of carrying out a risk assessment. However, you may find you want to produce a more sophisticated assessment. So long as you cover the recommended five steps, there is no reason why you can't do this. In fact, in the author's view, it helps to manage health and safety better.

 Author's advice

A risk assessment should be a working document that is revised on an ongoing basis. It is NOT something you do once and forget!

A good way of setting up a risk assessment is on the computer. You can buy specialist software packages, but all you need is a table or spreadsheet. This means that, you can change and add to your assessment all the time.

You can introduce a "hazard consequence" or "severity" rating column. If you grade the severity and the risk with numbers, say 1–5, you can multiply the two numbers and so get a risk score or rating factor.

Example:

Severity	x	Risk	=	Risk Score
3	x	2	=	6

The advantage of this system is it gives you a clear priority rating; the risks with the highest factor are the ones you have to address first. So if you have a risk rating of 5 and a severity rating of 5, your risk score would be 25. You have to do something drastic very quickly!

As mentioned under STEP 3, the control or risk reduction measures are the heart of your assessment. It is here where the real safety management takes place. You actions and conclusions must be relevant and appropriate to the risk.

The whole purpose of risk assessment is to eliminate or minimise the risk, not to find a "quick fix".

Hierarchy of control measures – don't go for the easy way out

Simply giving people **personal protective equipment** (**PPE**) or the **safety data sheets** is not exactly health and safety management. What you are required to do is **manage the hazard away** or, if that is not possible, reduce the risk.

There actually is a ranking order (hierarchy) of measures you must consider in effective health and safety management.

If you have identified a danger or hazard, the first thing you should try is to:

1. **Eliminate the hazard**, i.e. get rid of it.
    This could be achieved by either taking the dangerous object out of circulation, locking it away or repairing it.

    For instance, you discover one of the metal football goals on the pitch has rusted through at the cross bar, which would collapse if the ball hit it. It would therefore be unreasonable to carry on using this goal in its present state as it could cause injury to the children playing.

    Question: What are your options? The match is about to start.

    If you can't eliminate the hazard, then you try to:

2. **Replace the dangerous object or substance with another, less dangerous or harmless one** (this is called substitution).
    You could try and find another goal – if you have time! In some circumstances replacement is possible, e.g. you could replace a dangerous cleaning chemical with a less harmful one that does the same job. But replacement is not always possible, e.g. in a swimming pool, the biggest hazard is the water.

3. **Prevent access to hazard**
    As in point two, it works for certain things. Dangerous machines, hot or noisy objects can be put in separate rooms or guarded off.

4. **Reduce exposure to the hazard**
    You can do this by re-organising work, restricting access to authorized persons only, and limiting use of hazardous equipment to the minimum necessary.

5. **Minimise the risk**
    You can't eliminate or substitute the hazard; therefore you must try to reduce the risk of anything happening to a minimum possible.

    In our swimming pool example, we can't eliminate or replace or isolate the water, so we have to look at risk reduction.

    Question: How do you reduce the risk of people drowning?

6. **Issue personal protective equipment**
    This should only happen when all the above are not feasible. **PPE** is the last resort, not the first option!

7.   **Provide welfare facilities**
    For example, washing facilities to remove contamination or first aid.

It is important that you try and bear this ranking order in mind when deciding on your control measures. That way, you ensure you have acted in a responsible manner and have done everything to protect people in your care as far as reasonably possible.

Let's do a risk assessment!

On the following page is an example of a good risk assessment form. It shows you a couple of examples so you get the idea. Then you can have a go in the **Assessment activity 3**, but you may want to fill in a few rows now to get the hang of it.

 Author's advice

Make sure you include a key to you risk and severity rating,

e.g. for risk it could be 1 = low, 2 = fair, 3 = medium, 4 = high, 5 = very high

for severity:

> 1 = negligible injuries (cuts, nips)
>
> 2 = minor injuries (bruises, small concussions, fainting)
>
> 3 = debilitating injuries (bad concussions, small joint dislocations, minor fractures, ambulance called)
>
> 4 = serious injuries (severe bleeding, unconsciousness, hospitalisation, fractures of larger bones, dislocation of major joints, etc)
>
> 5 = fatality.

RISK ASSESSMENT FOR DODGY FOOTBALL CLUB

Hazard	Who is at risk?	Consequences of hazard. Severity 1=low, 5=high	Risk 1=low 5=high	Risk score SxR	Control measures	Monitor/review comments
Broken glass on pitch	All players	Severe cuts, infections 3	4	12	Thorough pitch inspection before each match. No glass allowed in stadium.	every 6 months. Also speak to bar staff and stewards
Stadium over capacity at top fixtures.	Spectators	Crushing leading to severe injuries and panic. 4/5	3	12–15	Tickets pre-sale for popular matches, tight control on spectator numbers, not to exceed capacity.	After each sell out match.

Don't assume that risk assessments are just for the sports facility; they have to be carried out for premises and equipment as well as activities because hazards can occur in all of them.

For instance, hazards could be

PREMISES:	Slippery sports hall floor, obstacles posing trip hazards, sharp or protruding edges.
EQUIPMENT:	Five-a-side goals not secured, trampoline not properly set up, frayed climbing ropes.
ACTIVITY:	Unsafe practices (bad tackles, diving in shallow end of pool), lack of control or supervision, allowing unsafe equipment.

Therefore, when you conduct a risk assessment, you should look at the actual premises or grounds, at the equipment available and the range of activities that take place in the premises and use of that equipment.

It is also very important that you consider your particular "audience"; a risk assessment for coaching a group of adults would look different from a risk assessment for younger children simply because of their age and vulnerability.

 Toolkit: Risk groups

Briefly list, in bullet points, how a beginners' swimming lesson for four- to six-year-old children would differ from a lesson for adults.

If you analyse the situation, you will find that the hazards are the same for the children and the adults (WATER – DROWNING).

The big risk actually lies in the **activity itself**, and the **group of people** who are at risk.

Adults are mature, they have the ability to understand instructions, they can control fear better and, hopefully, don't panic so quickly. They are also tall enough to stand in the water, which makes them feel safer. Therefore, your approach to teaching your swimming lesson safely is somewhat different for the two groups. For example, your teacher/pupils ratio is much higher for the children's class, and you may have helpers in the water with the children. Furthermore, you may have to ensure the water temperature is suitable for young children as they cool down much quicker than adults. Therefore:

1. Think of other high risk groups you could come across in a sports organisation or activity.
   How would this impact on your control measures?

2. Carry out a risk assessment for a Saturday afternoon fun session in a leisure pool. You allow children to bring balls and toys, and you also have a giant inflatable in the main tank.

Check out your sport!

See whether the National Governing Body of your own particular sport has issued any guidance or a code as to how to coach children and carry out a risk assessment. You can find out on the web.

 Tutor talk

If you're doing your **CSLA** or a coaching qualification, you will be required to carry out a risk assessment for your coaching session. Check with your tutor to see whether you can use the CSLA risk assessment for this unit.

Assessment activity 3: Risk assessment

LO 3:   Risk assessment

Risk assessment: How dodgy is Dodgy FC?

As the new operations manager of Dodgy FC you have already identified that there is no risk assessment at the club.

So you consider it high priority to carry out an assessment straight away to comply with the Management of Health and Safety at Work Regulations.

Task: Identify four different significant hazards and produce an accurate risk assessment using the above table format.

Your control measures should be specific, demonstrating that you have considered the hierarchy of measures (see page 220).

Section 4: Be secure – not just safe!

LO 4:   **Investigate the benefits to an organisation in effectively managing health, safety and security**

Like health and safety, security has become a serious issue with sports organisations. Badly managed security can lead to serious consequences. Clients and customers feel threatened and stay away, resulting in financial problems for the organisations.

For instance, if you knew a sports centre had a reputation for having cars on its car park broken into, would you consider parking your car there whilst playing squash?

But the problems can take on international dimensions. Just consider football hooliganism!

The England national football team was banned from playing in Europe for many years because of the reputation of its fans and was only allowed "back in" when it hosted the 1996 UEFA European Championship.

Each year, millions of pounds are spent on improving security at football grounds. Modern football stadiums like Old Trafford or Elland Road have special control rooms with sophisticated CCTV equipment that allows traffic flow and crowd behaviour to be monitored. Hundreds of stewards, security guards and policemen are involved in maintaining and monitoring security.

Security aspects for one-off events or activities largely depend on their nature (some attract more problems than others), their location, number of people attending and spectating, and other current issues such as the social or political environment.

At the Athens 2004 Olympic Games, security was paramount because of threats of terrorism in the wake of the Iraq War. Security for the Olympics is planned years ahead.

So you can see from these examples the importance organisations place on the management of safety and security. Although in day-to-day life, security does not generally face such big threats, it is important that you are aware of the problems facing modern sports organisations.

What are the security problems?

Toolkit: Figuring out security problems

Imagine you are the manager of a very large sports facility with dozens of staff and thousands of spectators/visitors.

What are the main threats to security facing you?

Try and think of the major problems and then categorise them in groups. You should be able to come up with at least four or five categories:

- _____

- _____

- _____

- _____

- _____

- _____

Answers (spelled backwards: ecneloiv, tfeht, duarf, msiladnav, egamad, misrorret, egatobas).

Toolkit: Sports history

Test your history of sports – try and find real life examples for each category during sporting events in recent years.

Notes

Violence – you must protect your staff

It Is your duty to ensure the security of your staff and customers, and protect them from violence and abuse. Although this may be difficult to implement sometimes, you must be able to show that you have reasonable and adequate measures in place to deal with foreseeable problems. You must not expose your staff to foreseeable threats of violence without any protection.

For instance, it would be unreasonable to have a junior female duty manager check a large inner city leisure centre at closing time late at night on her own.

Toolkit: Combat violence

Think of a sporting organisation and identify possible threats of violence to your staff and customers and implement measures to deal with them.

Possible threats	Measures
E.g. Receptionist threatened to hand money over.	CCTV, panic button, personal alarm, regular cash lifts, clear instructions for receptionist telling them what to do.

Theft and fraud

Theft can be of property, equipment, money and information/data. Fraud can take the shape of forged credit cards and "bouncing" cheques or counterfeit money, and staff forging records. The perpetrators could be outsiders to the organisation or they could be from within. The victims could be customers, staff or the organisation itself. Theft from the organisation and from staff can be particularly demoralising as it undermines the trust necessary in working with one another.

 Toolkit: Catch a thief

Now identify possible theft and fraud problems in your organisation.

Theft/fraud	Measures
From staff:	
From customers:	
From organisation:	

Damage and vandalism

Damage and vandalism can be a real problem. Damaged facilities and equipment can stop you from carrying out planned activities and, say, disrupt your programme. If you don't deal with these problems swiftly, they can rapidly escalate. You and your organisation will gain a bad reputation, which in turn will put off people using it. This could have serious consequences for the organisation.

 Toolkit: Stop the vandals

Now think what damage and vandalism problems you might have to deal with in a sports organisation.

Damage/vandalism	Measures
Property:	
Premises/facilities:	
Equipment:	

Terrorism and sabotage

These are the most dangerous security threats, but also the rarest. It does not mean you can ignore them because you might be involved in an organisation or a large event that could be the target of terrorists or saboteurs. Much depends on the national and international political situation at the time.

The 2004 Olympic Games were thought to be under a severe threat of terrorism because of the Iraq war; during the 1996 Olympic Games in Atlanta, a bomb went off. The most famous case of terrorism in sport happened during the 1972 Olympics in Munich, when Palestinensian terrorists killed several Israeli athletes.

Although it is unlikely that you will come across such a threat, it is important you are prepared should such a threat arise. You need to have procedures and systems in place so you and everybody affected know what to do.

"Safety in numbers" – managing crowds safely

One of the most important health, safety and security issues at large sporting events is crowd safety.

From the organiser's and club's point of view, large crowds are desirable because they boost income. But once a crowd gets out of control, there is not much you can do to stop it. Imagine the devastating effect of thousands of people panicking and trying to get out of a place, e.g. Hillsborough.

The key factor in crowd safety is **not to lose** control. Therefore, you should adopt a proactive approach to crowd safety. An effective team with clear roles and responsibilities and adequate training is important in this context.

Other preventative measures include site inspection, risk assessment, researching the type of crowd you are expecting, liaise with the police, etc.

The HSE recognised the importance of crowd safety many years ago, to the extent that it commissioned a study of crowd behaviour.

You can access the report and HSE guidance on managing crowds safely by going on to **www.hse.gov.uk/pubns/indg142.htm**.

Toolkit: Crowd management

Scenario

You are in charge of security at a Premier League football club that is expecting its local arch-rival. You are aware of the old animosity between the two clubs and the incidents that happened at previous matches.

1. Think of reasons why the crowd you expect could cause problems.
2. What could you do to control the crowd and stop the anticipated problems from occurring?

Security measures – yes, another assessment!

As with health and safety, the best way to manage security is to start with an assessment. Instead of safety hazards, you assess security hazards for the building, location, event or activity. You simply include the security risk assessment in you general risk assessment; the same format applies. (As a matter of fact, the HSE actually recommends including assessment of stress and violence to staff in your general risk assessment.)

Once you've identified the security hazards, think of who's at risk and the consequences if things go wrong. Then evaluate the risk and consider your security control measures.

 Toolkit: Security risk assessment

Using the format on page 220, carry out an assessment for at least one security problem in each category for a fictional or real sporting event. Here's an example of a security assessment for Formula One Grand Prix to start you off. Carry on with a few more!

Hazard	Who is at risk	Consequences of hazard. Severity 1=low, 5=high	Risk 1=low 5=high	Risk Score SxR	Control measures	Monitor/ review comment
E.g. Theft/pick pocketing	Spectators	3	3	9	Patrols by uniformed and under-cover stewards. Warning signs, CCTV.	

Good health and safety makes sound business sense

Organisations often do not see a direct, quantifiable benefit in health and safety, and are reluctant to spent time and money on it. Just imagine the consequences, though, of a fatality occurring during a Children's Activity due to lack of safety (in 2003, a teacher received a jail sentence because a child drowned during a school trip).

What would the consequences be for the organisation that was responsible for the tragedy? Think what would happen to customer numbers in a leisure centre if it developed a bad reputation for safety and hygiene. How would it make you feel if you worked in an unsafe environment or with unsafe equipment?

Toolkit: Benefits and consequences of good and bad health and safety

List the benefits of good and the consequences of bad health and safety for a sports organisation (for benefits and costs try **www.hse.gov.uk/costs**).

Benefits of good health and safety:

- _____

- _____

- _____

- _____

- _____

Consequences of poor health and safety:

- _____

- _____

- _____

- _____

- _____

Toolkit: Memo re benefits of good health and safety

You have just been employed by a local sports centre as a children's activity organiser, running after-schools clubs and holiday camps.

On checking out the sports hall and the equipment, you find that they do not meet your own safety standards. The manager tells you that there is no money in the budget to repair things or buy new equipment. You are also told that there is no other staff available to help you because of cut-backs and that you have to run activities involving 20 or more children on your own.

You are not happy with this and decide to write a memo outlining the consequences for the centre if an accident should occur. But you want to be positive and therefore want to stress the benefits of high safety standards in children's activities.

Write a memo to your manager not exceeding 300 words.

The memo's purpose is twofold:

1. To protect yourself from possible claims.

2. To persuade your manager that better health and safety is needed. Your manager is very commercially minded, therefore you have to make a sound case that the benefits of health and safety for the organisation outweigh the costs.

Author's advice

Your employer must not force you to do any job that might endanger yourself or others. You can refuse! But if you're worried about pressure, you should inform your boss how you feel, that you're not happy with things and that you feel pressurised doing that job. Do this in writing and keep a copy to cover yourself.

Tutor talk

You may wish to bring this up with your tutor and discuss it in class.

One shoe doesn't necessarily fit all

In a lot of cases, health, safety and security is a question of common sense and the general principles can be applied in most circumstances. But sometimes, more specific knowledge is required, particularly when dealing with specialist equipment or areas.

For example, sporting activities that are relatively complex such as pole vaulting or canoeing, or those that involve hazardous equipment like javelins or discuses, or those that are inherently dangerous like scuba diving or parachuting, demand in-depth knowledge and thought-out procedures. Also, specialist area such as physiotherapy, which requires a lot of training, or non-core activities like food and drink (you may have a bar/café on your premises) have to be carefully considered.

How do I get my message across?

There are several ways of getting your message across such as posters, leaflets, videos, training sessions, etc. First, though, you have to figure out who your target audience is, then you can devise the appropriate methods of reaching them.

Toolkit: Identify the best method of distribution

You're back at Dodgy FC As you already know, there are lots of things that need sorting out. From the list of things that you found wrong or missing on page 204, select some things that are badly wrong and determine who the specific groups are that you have to target with your message about better health, safety and security (remember, this may have to include the general public). For some guidance as to types of distribution, refer to your unit specification.

Once you have done that, try and figure out the best method of reaching those target groups. State the reason that you believe your chosen method would work.

Things that are wrong	Target group	Method	Reason
E.g.: Stewards watching the match and not the crowds.	Stewards	Regular training seminars, supervisors to reinforce instruction, correct behaviour when wrong, disciplinary action, induction and shadowing.	Need to understand their responsibilities and role, and what can happen if they do not fulfil their duty, need to be trained in appropriate responses.

Assessment activity 4: Benefits of health, safety and security

LO4:   Investigate the benefits of health, safety and security

Go check it out!

Select two sports organisation you know well.

1. Describe the benefits of managing health, safety and security for the two organisations.

2. Explain the effectiveness of the management of health, safety and security in the two organisations. In addition to your description, you now have to explain whether, and how well, health, safety and security is being managed.

3. Critically analyse the benefits of managing health, safety and security in the two organisations. This Building on your explanation in (2), you now must break health, safety and security management in the two organisations into its parts with comments and judgements. You should then draw conclusions and make recommendations as to how they could improve their management of health, safety and security. It might be helpful if you compared the two organisations.

Evaluating health, safety and security

Get feedback!

With health, safety and security, it is important that you monitor and review your control measures in order to find out whether they are working or not. You may have overlooked something, or not considered certain factors; as a result, your measures are not working as you intended.

This applies in particular to managing and promoting health and safety. You need to know whether your staff has understood what you were trying to get across to them, and whether they put that understanding into practice in their daily work routine. If you run a poster or leaflet campaign to raise awareness of health, safety and security, you will want to find out whether it has the desired effect. Otherwise, you could be wasting time and resources.

You should ask yourself a number of questions to help you ascertain whether your methods are working:

- Have I targeted the right audience?

- Have I chosen the best way to reach that audience, or are there better ways?

- Have I put the information in the right format, and in the right place?

- Are health, safety and security improving as a result of my efforts?

Ways of evaluating your promotional material, guidelines and channels of distribution include:

- questionnaires
- surveys
- focus groups and staff meetings
- observations
- inspections
- accident analysis.

Assessment activity 5: Produce guidelines for a target audience

Covering what the student has learned in this unit

Now it's time to put into practice what you have learnt so far. And see if you can put it all together by preparing guidelines for employees and customers.

1. Using your knowledge of health and safety, put together guidelines to help maintain a safe, secure and healthy sports environment.

2. Review the guidelines and explain the selected methods of distribution and evaluation. This means explaining your guidelines, why you have chosen them and how do you think they will help maintain health, safety and security.

3. Critically evaluate the guidelines, justifying the choice of distribution and evaluation procedures. This means, based on your review, try to be self-critical and examine the effectiveness of your guidelines, giving judgment as to why you think they will be effective. Further, you must then give good, logical reasons why you chose certain methods of distribution and evaluate them.